Ω

JAL WRITING

Spring Lake, NJ

Printed by CreateSpace. 2014

ISBN   978-0-615-94779-2

Cover photograph by John Ozell

Cover designed by David Anthony Maietta

Is the Devil Winning?

By

John A. Leonard

Dedicated to the love of my life - Sheree. Without your love and encouragement this would have never been possible.

To my family who has always given me so much love and support

and

To Alyson Payan, who will always be my little angel. Know that if you follow your dreams they can one day become a reality.

Special thanks to Daniel Nelms, executive pastor of the Remedy Church in Brick Township, NJ.

"If you dance with the devil, you don't get to choose the music."

CONTENTS

It was going to be one of those September days. Warm, but not hot, the sun shining brilliantly in the sky. Summer had a couple of weeks left and it was ready to make sure it left us with at least one more beautiful day. A gorgeous day, but life continued as it normally does. The subways in New York City were packed with the morning rush. The highways into Washington D.C. were jammed with people trying to get to work. It was just like every other weekday. Kisses goodbye were given. Plans for the night were made. The stock market was poised for another strong day. The good days just kept on coming. It seems that mankind is easily fooled into believing the good times are going to last forever. Instead of enjoying days like this we tend to take them for granted. We think that they are our God-given right instead of a gift we should enjoy and be thankful for. It's almost like man has the uncanny quality to forget the bad times and only focus on the good. An uncanny trait for sure, but perhaps a bad quality that man possesses.

Always keeping our eyes on the prize without watching out for the roadblocks in our way. It is a trait that leads man to great successes. We keep the goal in sight and when we reach it the feeling is incredible. Unfortunately for us, there is also a flip side to the coin we call life. When the flip side of the coin comes up, which it inevitably will, it all too often slaps us when we least expect it and the result is much harsher than it should have been. But the sun was out and the temperature was perfect. It sure was looking like it was going to be another beautiful day.

The time was 8:45 in the morning. The date was September 11, 2001. The day, which seemed so ideal to many, was not ideal to the passengers on four planes. It must have been hell. A hell which they were continually being told would be over soon if they cooperated. Mohammed Atta told the passengers of Flight 11, a flight he and three others had just hijacked, that everything was going to be fine if they listened to his orders to stay seated. They were going to land and give their demands to end this horror. Perhaps the passengers believed the hijacker. This was how hijacked planes turned out- right? The plane returned to the airport, the hijackers negotiated, and then either surrendered or were killed. It would be many hours of terror and tension, but in the end all would get resolved. This was not going to be one of the "normal" hijackings. September 11th, 2001, was the day that would change how we looked at things and how we viewed life in general. That day, I believe, the question first started to fester in people's minds. Is the devil winning? I am sure everyone believed this was the work of the devil but this was more than they had ever seen. The tide, perhaps, was turning.

The clock hit 8:46 AM on the East Coast of the United States. Flight 11, which had been flying way too low and way too fast, was in Lower Manhattan. Atta was not confused about how to get to JFK airport. He knew exactly what he has doing. The North Tower of the World Trade Center glistened in the ever decreasing distance. The time for evasive action was long past as the 767 jet was travelling at well over 400 MPH. Mohammed Atta stayed the course and the world was about to undergo a terrifying change. Flight 11, with a full supply of jet fuel, barreled into the Tower destroying floors 93 to 99. The passengers and crew of the flight were instantly killed as well as scores of people in the tower. The plane also caused severe damage to the building's core. President Bush was visiting a school in Florida. When told of the crash of Flight 11, he thought what many people thought- "What a tragedy" and "What was that pilot thinking?" The thought of a terrorist attack had not yet begun to percolate in our mindset. The mainland of the United States, after all, had not seen a foreign attack in any of our lifetimes. Terrorism was something we heard about on the news, usually in some faraway place few Americans could pronounce. It did not happen here. Never.

Those watching the terror as it began to unfold on television did not have long to think that a poor pilot caused the crash into the north tower. They watched the smoke plumes coming from the building and prayed for the poor souls that had perished. Seventeen minutes had passed since flight 11 hit the north tower. The event had been televised live for about ten minutes. The television coverage, for ten minutes at least, was consistent with how events like this were covered. True, a jet liner had never flown into a skyscraper, but with all the giant buildings in the city it was bound to eventually happen. Right?

Any day before this they might have been correct. It would have been decompression in the cabin that caused this terrible accident. It would have been...anything other than what it actually was. It was now 9:02 A.M., eastern daylight time.

United Flight 175 was the second plane to be hijacked that day. Its target was the same as Atta's- the World Trade Center. It was without a doubt already a monumental event. Terrorists had been able to infiltrate the United States, hijack a plane, and fly it full speed into the tallest building in a city full of giant buildings. Perhaps the hijacker was emboldened when he saw the smoke and flames coming from the North Tower. Atta's plan had worked. The hijacker took aim and jammed down on the throttle. At speeds nearing 600 MPH, flight 175 smashed into the South Tower, once again killing all on board and countless others in the tower. This event was caught live on most of the major television networks. Screams from the people looking up as the plane crashed were recorded. Those on the Eastern coast and the middle of the United States now knew the fantasy was over. This was no accident. It had quickly become something that no American thought they would live to see.

America was under attack. Four words that we never thought we would ever hear. We lost some good men at Pearl Harbor, but Hawaii was in the Pacific and not in the American heartland. We had undergone the Cold War and its constant threat of nuclear warfare unscathed. We thought we were in for a lifetime of good days. Two planes had smacked that idea out of us.

September 11th, 2001, continued as chaotic as it had started. The west coast awakened to the nightmare in process- the headlines on the television screamed, "AMERICA UNDER ATTACK!" The news stations called it an act of terrorism, but that was not what the people were worried about. We were worried about what was still to come. The next few hours did little to relieve the worry of the American people. American Airlines Flight 77- a Boeing 757- smashed into the Pentagon. The Pentagon! The headquarters for the U.S. military had been attacked. The question then became how bad this day would end up being and whether the attacks were finished. A half hour after the Pentagon was hit, United Flight 93 crashed in Pennsylvania after passengers of the plane tried to storm the cockpit to regain control from the hijackers. Although we did not know it then, that was the last of the hijacked planes. Unconfirmed reports stated there were more planes unaccounted for and presumed hijacked. The devil, having begun the day spreading terror and blood, was about to unleash another part of his arsenal- fear of the unknown. It is a weapon that the devil often uses against man, but on this day he set up things to ensure that the fear of mankind would be strong. He ensured that it would be long lasting. Once again, the devil was testing the resolve of mankind and the strength of God.

The South Tower of the World Trade Center collapsed at 9:58 AM and the North Tower fell a half an hour later. When the South Tower collapsed, I was driving to my job and listening to the events on the radio. I had to pull the car over. I just could not believe that the 110 story building was now gone. Now that I had received my smack in the face, I was expecting the worst. When the second tower fell, I was more upset than shocked. Like all Americans I was mad that someone had the gall to attack us and also worried about what would be next. When the smoke from the collapsed buildings finally cleared, the southern tip of the island of Manhattan resembled a post-apocalyptic movie set.

The bright and vivid colors that were the city were now negated by the soot caused by the destruction of the buildings. People who had escaped the carnage were covered in soot and looked ghostly. The news coverage did its best to stay away from showing gruesome scenes, but the images they did show were more than enough. This was no movie set. This was no dream. Although we did not know the number then, we now know that 2,977 people who started their day like it was any other were no longer with us.

As with most events of this magnitude, the United States did not have the time to curl up in a corner and mourn its losses. The fact remained that we were attacked. The fact remained that thousands of people were now gone. There were memorial concerts, presidential first pitches, chants of USA, and many tears. President Bush said we would not rest until those responsible and those protecting them were brought to justice and we believed him. We were told Usama bin Laden was the mastermind behind the attacks and that he was hiding behind the Taliban in Afghanistan and we wanted him dead. The American people were told that bin Laden's terror group Al

Qaeda carried out the attacks and we wanted it destroyed. Then September 11th became October 11th and there were no more attacks on America. The year 2001 came to an end. Americans, ever resilient, were settling into the new "normal". There was the ever present fear that terror would raise its ugly head again but we were ready now. That evil would never show its face on our soil again.

After the terrorist events of 9/11, the devil must have sat back with a sick grin. He had put two of his weapons together and successfully unleashed them on man. Fear and anger. Used separately they are formidable. Together they are damn near impossible to defeat. The devil, of course, knew this from his previous failures at crushing the spirit of mankind. I will never say the devil is smart, but I will say that he has a fierce mind for all things that are evil. He would wait. As much as the devil hates waiting, he must have known he had set the stage up for future evils. The fear and anger would fester. The devil would unleash another one of his weapons when man was unsuspecting and most vulnerable- greed. The sick grin turned into an evil chuckle. Humans, as unsuspecting and gullible as ever, were primed for an attack. The game was on. As always, it was a game that the ever prideful devil expected to win. It must be remembered that the free will of man is able to reject the devil and his evil ways. The battle between God and the devil may or may not be upon us, but the devil is always looking for more souls to recruit to his side.

It is amazing to look at how the public's view of "the devil" has changed through time. The image has gone from a demonic beast with horns, cloven feet, a spiked tail, and a pitchfork to an almost cuddly little imp with a naughty smile on his face. Fear of the devil seemed to be limited to loud mouthed televangelists, Bible belt preachers, and grandmas from the old country. Perhaps I am exaggerating. Maybe we are able to realize that this "commercial" and cute image of the devil is different than the pure evil that we know to be the devil. It could have been, of course, that we as man lost our fear of the devil. It may very well have been we started to give the devil a blind eye and began to blame God for all of the evils of the world. What many people tend to forget is that the devil is a fallen angel. Every image we have is simply an image from man's imagination. We cannot know what the devil looks like, but I am sure that even the fall could not cause the devil to change from his angelic look to a cloven beast. He may very well look like you or me.

The question, "Is the Devil Winning?" was once both taboo and unimaginable. Simply uttering the phrase with any seriousness would cause a person to be labeled as either an atheist or a devil worshipper. It was not considered a legitimate or acceptable question. The question would likely get someone ostracized- if not worse. It was a theme throughout history that the forces of evil and the devil were a nasty reality that man would have to deal with before the forces of good and God conquered and vanquished the evil. The events of September 11th started a change in the view of the question. Yes, this was an act of war, but it was unlike any other event that we had seen before. It was everything that people said it was- an evil, cowardly act. Yet, it was allowed to happen and the terrorists who carried out the attacks were both thriving and continuing to perform heinously evil acts. Years passed and the world and the threat of terror did not to seem to improve or ease. The fear and anger began to swell and the question started to be asked by the mainstream. Those who started to ask the question were not called atheists or devil worshippers. The question was being asked by Mom and Pop. It was being asked by the neighbor next door. It was being asked by us.

The thought to write this book first appeared in my mind a few years ago. I wrote a few pages and then put it aside. Things would get better. They had to. I moved to other creative pursuits. I began writing screenplays and I have four finished sitting on my bookcase. I was able to make it to the quarterfinals of a screenplay competition with one of my works. Perhaps screenwriting is the path my creative juices will eventually follow, but there was still something lingering in the back of my mind. Years had passed but things had not gotten much better. The question was still being asked. The thought was still in people's minds. It had not gotten any weaker- if anything it had grown. The question itself is not as simple as the four words it contains. It is a deep question that not only asks if the devil (evil) is conquering God (good). If one looks even deeper, it can be argued that perhaps this question is the harbinger for the end of times. It could be argued that the devil is building his strength for his attack on the gates of Heaven. There are many things that this question could mean and none of them are good.

As I type these words, I understand the enormity of the topic I am about to undertake. I also understand that my shortcomings as a human being make what I am about to write simply the musings of a weak mortal. Knowing that I could never understand the works of God or His fallen angel makes this a bit easier. I will not be prophesizing doom and gloom and making bold predictions. I also will not try to paint a rosy picture and tell you that everything is fine. We will examine the history of the devil in theology. We will study some of the current events that have led people to seriously question whether the devil is gaining power. I will also give my answer to the question that gives the title to this book as well as gives so many people an uneasy, worried feeling. Is the devil winning?

The concept of good and evil has existed throughout time. Whatever side you are on (or off) religiously, it cannot be denied that there is a definite schism between what is good in the world and what is evil. It is fortunate that the good things always seem to greatly outweigh those things we deem to be bad. Whenever evil would raise its ugly head, good would rally and end up triumphant. The one thing history seemed to teach us is that no matter how bad things may seem the forces of good will always conquer. It would be a long and exhausting process to go into detail on all the historical instances of evil and the various forms attributed to evil. The history of mankind is flooded with examples of the evils of the devil. As much as I know I will give up on a task like that, I also know you will give up reading. I do not want either to happen. We cannot explore fully the question "Is the devil winning?", however, without first looking at some historical and theological examples of the devil at work. So without any further ado, let's travel back to ancient times and to the time of Jesus and look at the history of evil and the devil.

With a few exceptions, religion in ancient times took on a polytheistic nature. The names of the gods of the ancient Greeks and Romans stay with us to this day. They are now the names of our planets. They are now corporate logos. Though the world has transformed to a mostly monotheistic tone, it is interesting to see how the gods of ancient times still have a presence even though they are no longer worshipped. Today, the monotheistic religions of Christianity and the Muslim faith are practiced by more than half of the world's population. We will focus on the works on the devil in those faiths later in this section as they provide a clearer look at the devil as we view him today. As a Christian, I believe that the devil has always been a part of the Earth. I also believe it is important to see how the devil worked his evil in ancient religions in order to help us come up with an answer for this book's question. The religious history of Ancient Egypt will provide us with a good look at an ancient religion and how the devil was also present in this polytheistic society.

We, in modern times, are intrigued by the ancient civilizations that preceded us. The literary works of Plato,

Socrates, and of course the pyramids of Egypt leave us in wonder. Ancient Egypt proved itself to be an engineering giant that was way before its time. This fact has led some to claim that all the wonders of Ancient Egypt were in fact the work of extraterrestrial influences. I do not believe that, nor will I pay it any more attention. The pyramids the Egyptians built, as well as the sphinx, are still standing and leave us in astonishment. What were the religious beliefs of a society able to build such magnificent monuments that still stand today? We now know that the pyramids were to be the final resting place of the Pharaoh before moving to the afterlife. The hieroglyphics of the ancient Egyptians have taught us that the society had a complex religious system that included many gods and goddesses. With such a collection of idolatry, it would seem that a god who promoted evil would be inevitable. Enter Set, the god of darkness and confusion, and a mythological figure that would survive until the ancient Greeks who renamed him Seth. As a god who represented such qualities, Set most resembles the devil we know today.

When one thinks of the religion and mythology of the Ancient Egyptians few would believe that it has any connections to the modern monotheistic religions of the modern world. They did, after all, worship numerous gods, worshipped the sun, and believed Pharaohs to be divine. It would be easy to set aside their beliefs as those of an ancient and primitive people. Many people today would prefer to brush the Ancient Egyptian religion aside and continue to believe that these were an ancient people and not as wise as the modern man. That would be an easy "out" many people today would choose. Easy- yes- but exactly what does this accomplish? There is a saying about those who forget the past are doomed to repeat it. While I do not mean to say that we will become polytheistic sun worshippers, I do think it is important to know the past and how we got to where we are. The religion of the ancient Egyptians may have similarities to modern religions and I believe that it is important for us to look at their god of evil.

When writing about a polytheistic religion, it can be easy to get lost or at the very least get off track. With the focus being the history of the devil, it allows us to narrow the gap down to a handful of gods. Osiris, Isis, Horus, and Set give us the best example of the divine battle between good and evil in the Ancient Egypt religion. Osiris and Isis were husband and wife as well as brother and sister and represented the good in Egyptian life. Osiris was a god of grain and the Nile River, both of which were essential to the Egyptian people. Isis was the goddess of green crops and abundance. If we would stop at this point, the religious beliefs of ancient Egypt would seem to us like every other polytheistic religion. The people prayed for a bountiful harvest that would give them what they needed. In return, they would worship and give sacrifices. At first glance, it definitely seems like the Egyptian religion closely followed the polytheistic religions of ancient times. We have already said, however, that with the Pyramids the Egyptians were well beyond their time technologically. So why would their religious beliefs not be the same?

While it would seem with just a quick glance that the gods and goddesses of Ancient Egypt only represented the major essential needs of the Egyptian civilization, a deeper look shows that the religion started advancing along with the culture.

Re, the sun god, was the father of both Osiris and Isis, and his wife Nut, through a secret affair, gave birth to Set. Osiris is the god that moved the Ancient Egyptian theology away from the common polytheistic religions of the time. Osiris was both human and god. As the god of the Nile, his human form ebbed and flowed with the status of the river. Droughts in this desert country were not uncommon, and Osiris would suffer and ultimately die as the river dried. As uncommon a thing as a god in a polytheistic religion dying is, the rest of the story of Osiris is even more uncommon. Osiris and Isis- brother and sister, husband and wife- had a son named Horus. Horus, as both son of man and son of a god, also had the unique ability to raise the dead. It was the adoration of Horus that gave the ancient Egyptians hope that they could be granted entrance into the afterlife with Osiris.

As this book is about the devil, let us now talk of the god who exemplified evil in the ancient Egyptian society- Set. A half-brother to Osiris, Set was the god for everything Osiris was not. Whereas Osiris was the god of the life giving Nile, Set was the god of the relentless Sahara desert. Osiris' father was the sun god while Set was the god of darkness and confusion. The stage was set for a good old battle between the forces of good and the forces of evil. Set would focus his energy on attacking his half-brother Osiris- the "chosen" son of the gods. While the Egyptian people did not exactly label Set as the god of evil, the writings about the gods clearly establish a good versus evil story line. The battle lines, as they say, were established. "Good" was represented by Osiris, Isis, and Horus and Set was the main evil component who would continually torment his "good" counterparts. The stories of evil in ancient Egyptian times do follow a modern theme. Set, no matter how devious and evil, could never fully defeat Osiris. On the other hand, Osiris and Horus could never truly defeat Set. Good would always conquer evil, although evil could never truly be vanquished. Sound familiar?

The stories of Set follow our beliefs on the tactics that evil uses in its attacks on the forces of good. Set never launched a forward attack against his fellow gods. He used deception, trickery, and lies in his attempts to overthrow the forces of good. An example of this is when Set was able to trick and kill Osiris.

Although he was ultimately unsuccessful in destroying "good", the story shows all the ways evil tries to conquer and overcome what is considered good in life. Osiris traveled Egypt teaching the people sophisticated ways of farming, established laws, and taught the people how to worship the gods. Osiris was successful in creating a more civilized Egyptian society and he decided to travel throughout the world in an attempt to convert people to accept his ideas. When he was away trying to spread his message, Set saw his opening. He wanted to take over Egypt. He wanted the people to worship him. Although he looked for any opportunity to rise above Osiris in his absence, he was closely watched by Isis and did not have an opportunity. Set, like the evil we have come to know, bided his time until Osiris returned from his journeys. Upon Osiris's return Set unleashed his plan to destroy the god of the Nile once and for all.

Set would use the power of evil to trick Osiris into a trap. Once more it was shown that evil did not have the power to attack that which is good, but had to resort to underhanded tactics during battle. Set secretly measured Osiris's body and had an ornate box built that would perfectly fit the body of the god of the Nile. He was also able to convince seventy-two of Osiris's followers to join him and revolt against the god Osiris. The plotting complete, Set just needed to execute his plan. He invited Osiris and the followers who had fallen for his tricks to a feast. After the feast Set brought out the box he had built to the admiration of all the guests. This was expected by Set and he stated that if anyone fit in the box perfectly he would give them the box. Of course, none of the conspirators were able to fit perfectly. Osiris tried the box and found himself a perfect fit. The conspirators then jumped to action, grabbing the box's cover and nailing it down. Molten lead was then poured over the box to ensure the death of the man/god. The box was placed in the Nile and Osiris was left to drift from existence.

Word of the treachery of Set spread and quickly got to Isis. She mourned the loss of Osiris and was determined to find the box that contained her love. Isis wandered throughout Egypt searching for Osiris's remains. She finally located the box in the palace of a king and entered the palace as nurse for the queen. Isis bided her time as nurse of one of the queen's sons before eventually revealing her story. The queen allowed her to retrieve the box and Isis brought it back to a remote part of the Egyptian desert. Once there, she opened the box and sobbed over the body of her deceased husband. The story then follows what would be considered polytheistic lore- Isis got bird wings and flapped air for Osiris to breathe and said some magic words to bring him back to life. This only lasted a short time, but it was long enough for Isis to become pregnant with Osiris's son Horus.

As Horus grew, he would be the one charged with revenging his father's death and destroying Set. When Osiris was certain that Horus was ready, he taught him how to use ancient weapons and set him forth on his quest to get revenge against Set. Horus and Set fought three epic battles. Each battle was hard fought but each time Horus emerged as the winner. Despite being vanquished, Set could never be completely destroyed. The good of the world had conquered but the evil could not be destroyed. Set accepted Horus's right to rule, and Horus returned the land to peace and prosperity. As Horus was born from his deceased father's seed, he was also named judge of the dead before they gained entrance into the afterlife. Besides the peace and prosperity Horus had brought the people, he also gave them an opportunity to gain life in the other world. The Egyptian religion now provided its people a greater reason than simply providing the bare necessities for their good deeds. With Horus being the judge that allowed them entrance into the afterlife, the Egyptian people now had an even greater purpose to strive for.

Through our quick glance at the Egyptian beliefs, we are able to make a few assumptions about their religion and ancient polytheistic religions in general. The ancient religions seem to have been based on the natural resources a people need to survive. Good were the gods who provided them with bountiful harvests and calm weather. Evil were the gods who blocked the sun or made the weather relentless and caused the necessary farming to be difficult. These can be seen by the conflicts between Osiris, Isis, Horus and Set. One side contained the gods of the Nile and of green plants, the other the god of darkness and confusion. As the forces of good and bad were attuned to the survival of the society, it was less of a religious belief as opposed to a necessity belief. If the crops were not growing, if it was not raining enough, the gods were mad at them. In the case of the Egyptians, it could be said that Set was spreading darkness and confusion over Egypt. The Egyptians, however, moved their polytheistic religion a step further with their belief that through Horus they would be able to gain entrance into the afterlife. If nothing else, the Egyptians set the stage for the monotheistic religions of today.

While not in historical time order, we will nevertheless enter the world of monotheistic religions with the Islamic faith. The religion dates back to about the sixth century AD, and is based on the belief and worship of Allah. The Qur'an, also called the Koran, is the religious text for all the followers of the Islamic religion. It is believed to have been the product of over twenty years of prophesies to the prophet Mohammed. Today, the Islamic faith has about one and a half billion followers, making it the second most followed religion in the world. For our intents and purposes, we will focus our attention on the Qur'an and its teachings about the devil, or as they call it- Iblis. As the Qur'an was written centuries after both the Torah and the Christian Bibles, there are some similarities between the religious texts. The belief of both the Christian Bible and the Islamic Qur'an is that the devil is a fallen angel. It is a hotly contested dispute as to whether Iblis was actually an angel or if he was a jinn. We will continue as though Iblis is a fallen angel as he is mentioned as part of the angels early in the book. Although in each of the texts the devil will eventually fall when the time of judgment comes, the paths that the two devils take on is quite different. Let us now talk about Iblis, the fallen angel of the Islamic faith.

The first mention of a fallen angel occurs early in the Qur'an. Allah created Adam and anointed him his deputy on Earth. He had Adam name all the angels, and commanded them to kneel before him. The angels all obeyed Allah with the exception of Iblis. He was overtaken by pride and refused to bow before man. This pride caused Iblis to immediately become an unbeliever in Allah. Adam was sent to Paradise to live with his wife and enjoy all the gifts that Allah had given to him. The only thing Allah commanded was that Adam not eat the fruit of a forbidden tree. Iblis, of course, saw his opportunity. He lured

Adam and his wife to eat from the forbidden tree and caused their banishment from Paradise. Although Allah banished Adam from Paradise, he showed mercy upon man by giving Adam his commandments and a promise that whoever follows his guidance would have nothing to fear when they die.

The story of Iblis and the fall of man is told in further detail later in the Qur'an. Allah asks Iblis why he did not bow before Adam when commanded to do so. The devil, in all his pride, responded that he was nobler than man. Allah, of course, knew that the pride in his fallen angel could not be allowed to stay in paradise. Iblis was banished from the angels to give him humility. He asked Allah for a reprieve which the Merciful Allah granted until the day of resurrection. Iblis then said he would walk the Earth tempting man away from Allah's straight path to prove that they are not worthy of the love of the Lord. The devil believes that he will find more that transgress than those who follow the commandments of Allah. Paradise, however, is saved for the true believers who reject the temptation of Iblis while those who transgress and fall for the devil's tricks will suffer in the fires of hell. When those transgressors fall and look to Iblis for help he will be powerless.

In the Qur'an, Iblis never begs Allah for forgiveness nor does he look to overtake the kingdom of Allah. The pride of the devil is too much for that. He is content to use every trick imaginable to coerce Allah's people away from his teachings before the days of judgment when he will enter the fires of hell. As Iblis never had any belief that he is greater than Allah or any desire to take over control of the kingdom, his goal is simply to prove that he was right in saying that the angels were nobler than mankind. He would attack the souls of mankind at every opportunity he had. It would begin with the whispers to Adam. The one thing in paradise that Adam could not enjoy was the fruit of the forbidden tree, and Iblis used that to his advantage. As Iblis knew that Allah had made man with free will, he knew that his powers of deception could sway man against following Allah's commandments. This was the first test of man and Iblis was able to easily sway human thought into craving that which Allah told him he could not possess.

For followers of the Islamic faith, it is a daily battle to fight the whispers and the temptations of Iblis and to follow Allah's straight path. It is a struggle that the followers of Allah will have to fight until the days of judgment. Remember, there will be no struggle for supremacy when that time comes. Iblis was given reprieve until then and will be sent to hell along with those foolish enough to allow the devil and his pride to lead them off the path of righteousness. Those who are able to resist the tricks and temptations of the devil will gain entrance into paradise. The faithful will be rewarded with everlasting life, while those who stray from the straight path are condemned to eternity in the flames of hell. The path to everlasting life in paradise is quite clear to the followers of Allah. Followers are simply asked to praise and worship Allah and remain on his straight path. As we well know, however, man is all too often unable or unwilling to avoid the whispers of the devil and have set themselves up to join Iblis in hell when the end of days comes.

Before we make an analysis of the Islamic view on the devil, let us first study the view of Christianity on the devil.

With over two billion followers, the Christian faith is the largest religion in the world. The holy work of the Christian faith is the Bible. Christianity is a continuance of Judaism with Christians believing that the Messiah promised by God was delivered to them by Jesus of Nazareth. Jesus, the Son of God, suffered, was crucified, and died. Christians believe that Jesus rose from the dead and will return at the End of Days to judge the living and the dead for entrance in God's Kingdom. As the Christian faith had its start centuries before the Islamic faith, there are many similarities between the holy works of the two faiths. The Qur'an has many of the same characters, but the views held in each work are very different- even the views of the devil are in stark contrast. The evil that consumes the devil and the tricks and deception he uses against man is never questioned. Now, as our last look at the history of the devil in theological literature, let us delve into the devil as described in the Christian Bible.

The Bible begins with the story of creation. God created the Heavens and the Earth and all of the creatures that inhabit the earth. On the sixth day of creation, God created man in His image. He gave man dominion over all the vegetation and animal life He created. The first man, Adam, was placed in the

Garden of Eden- a paradise on Earth- where he could enjoy and eat of all the plant life with the exception of the fruit from the tree of knowledge of good and evil. The Lord created a mate for Adam from his rib and man and woman would share their company in the Paradise of Eden. The first view of the devil also occurs early in the Christian Bible. The devil tempted the woman to eat of the fruit from the forbidden tree. He used trickery and leaned on the free will that God had given man to lure her to eat of the fruit of the tree. The woman then gave the fruit to Adam and he also ate the fruit of the forbidden tree. The original sin of mankind was now complete. Mankind had gone against the will of God and was forever banished from the Paradise of Eden. The stage was set early in the Christian Bible. The Book of Genesis clearly places God as good and all powerful, the devil as evil and conniving, and man as a vulnerable being. All this occurs in the first few pages of the Bible and sets the stage for a fierce battle between the forces of good and that of evil.

In the book of Job, Satan once again challenges the faith of man and their allegiance to God. Satan sneaks his way into God's presence, and for the purpose of this book I feel it better to translate the Bible into a more modern tone. When God sees Satan in His presence he asks the fallen angel, "Where did you come from?" The devil, in his irreverent style, responds by saying he's been here and there and just walking the Earth. Knowing the devil's opposition to man and his doubts about their loyalty, God asks the devil if he had considered Job as a loyal follower of God's ways. Job is described in the Bible as a God-fearing man who despises evil. As such, he is rewarded with family and property that makes him the greatest man in the east. The devil makes the claim that Job is only loyal because of all that he has been given. He asks God to allow him to take away his happiness and worldly goods to see whether Job will still be an upright man afterwards. God agrees with the only stipulation being that Job's life is safe.

The first tribulations that Job endured were the loss of his physical and monetary property, and the deaths of his sons. His wife says he should curse God but Job responds to this by saying he should not curse God- he should receive the bad as well as the good. The devil, though, is not done with Job. He placed upon Job a horrible disease that affected Job's skin and, as we would put it, made his life a living hell. Job cursed his life, but not God directly. He cursed the day he was born and said that God should have never allowed his birth to occur. The rest of the Book of Job has Job questioning the actions of God, but Job never curses God. At the end of the Book, God reveals Himself before Job. He directly answers all of Job's questions on his tribulations and asks Job who is man to question the works of God. Job immediately realizes the error of his ways and drops to his knees to repent. His tribulations now finished without cursing God, Job was given more monetary property than before and lived a long life. The book of Job, as opposed to the fall of man in the Garden of Eden, shows us that even failed mortals can reject the evils of the devil. Job may have questioned God but he was not foolish enough to curse or reject the Lord.

The Christian Bible moves from the Old Testament to the New Testament with the introduction of the long awaited Savior Jesus. Jesus was sent to Earth to open the gates of Heaven for mankind. With that being said, and with Jesus being both man and God, it should come as no surprise that the devil would try to tempt Jesus and take him away from his divine quest. Perhaps this is the most brazen example of the devil trying to overtake God and the forces of good. Knowing how weak man is the devil moves on his chance to tempt Jesus while He is still in His human form. The attempt by the devil to make God sin is so important to the New Testament that the first attempt appears in the first book of the New Testament and in the first chapters of that book. As we finish our look at the theological history of the devil, let us begin our New Testament research by looking at the Gospel of Matthew, Chapter 4, where the devil tempts Jesus in the desert.

Something that topples the will of man is seeking the temptation of sin. It is all too often that we enter situations that we know are likely to lead us into sin and it is part of our failings as human beings. We want more and more and do not consider the circumstances or ultimate outcome on our soul. Matthew gives us a delicate situation for Jesus. As God, he knows that the devil will try to tempt him in the desert. He also knows if he goes on his own for this temptation that as a man He will have sinned. The Holy Spirit therefore led Jesus into the desert so he could confront and refute the temptations of the devil. In the Gospel of Matthew, this occurs right after the baptism of Jesus. God knew that Jesus had to face the devil and his evils and deception to know what He would be facing as He continued his earthly mission to save the souls of man. Jesus fasted in the desert for forty days and when finished He of course hungered. The devil saw his opportunity and tempted Jesus to make bread from stones. When that failed to tempt Jesus, the devil then used the failings of man which we know as pride and greed. He tempted Jesus to leap from the temple and then to join him to take over the world. Jesus would reject the temptations of the devil each time and the devil was forced to give up and left Jesus. As we saw in the Book of Genesis, the devil was easily able to conquer the spirit of man. Here, the devil was unable to even lure God into sin, even though Jesus was also a human at the time.

In the Qur'an, Iblis waits for the End of Days and when it comes he accepts his fate and is sent to the flames of hell. The devil in Christianity does not accept that fate. We have seen that the devil in the Christian Bible not only continually tempts man but he also attempts to trick God. The Book of Revelation teaches us that the Christian devil does not accept this fate and details what will happen to the devil in those final days. The Bible details what seems to us to be the chaotic events that will lead to God conquering and imprisoning the devil after a war in heaven between the forces of good and the forces of evil. The devil is never shown to have a chance. In no part does the devil even seem to have the upper hand over God. The Revelation of St. John the Divine is the only book in the New Testament that focuses on prophecies and it works to finish the story started with the devil first waging his war of good versus evil in the Book of Genesis.

Our quick study of the history of the devil in theological terms shows us a number of things not only about the devil but also about the change that has occurred in the views of humans towards their religious beliefs. As we saw in the Egyptian polytheistic religion, the religion is based upon being good to ensure that the gods provided them with the resources necessary for their survival on Earth. A god of green crops. A god of the life giving river. Although the Ancient Egyptian faith started to grow and embrace the theme of everlasting life, in its core it was still a faith based upon the needs of its people. As we went forward into the monotheistic religions, God was still the one who provided man with all the necessary resources to survive. That, however, was not the key essence that people looked for with their religion. Both Islam and Christianity offer their followers a chance at eternal life in Paradise. It is an offer that no one would turn down, yet many fail to perform the most basic tasks that are needed to gain entrance to Paradise. That is where the devil comes into play. The evil that the devil spreads throughout mankind can be difficult to withstand. As Adam and Eve fell in the Garden of Eden, we as humans continue to fall to his trickery. It is a battle humans will have to fight until the end of times.

The Bible and the Qur'an both provide man with the ultimate resolution being the power of good conquering the forces of evil and the devil. Despite this, people still wonder if the forces of evil are overcoming those of good. It is apparent that the devil is still using his tricks of lies and deception to pull on the threads of the free will that was given to us by our God. The question that we need to ask ourselves then is why are we now so concerned with the devil winning the battle? For the followers of the world's two largest religions, the answer is spelled out in their religious texts. Iblis will accept his fate and the Devil will be conquered by God's angels. Despite this, even in the hearts of the faithful the question persists. Is this the work of the devil casting doubts in us? Is it that the events of our current time are unlike any we have experienced before? Or is it the unthinkable- is the devil really winning?

Thus far we have spent the entire book asking the question and describing the history of the devil in theological terms. It was important to do so before we even made an attempt to try to answer the question. Now that we have some historical background on the spiritual history of the devil and his evil, it is time to look at some of the current events that have brought upon the worried looks and thoughts of people today. It is without question that the events of our age are very different than any other that mankind has had to face. Therefore, we will now discuss some of the major issues that people think are the signs that the devil is winning. Hopefully at that point we will be able to come up with as good a response as mere mortals can to the question "Is the devil winning?"

Evil has always been a part of the human existence. Even when we were simple hunters and gatherers, our free will and pride has always caused us to want more. It is an inherent flaw of man and the flaw that the devil has used from his initial temptation of man in the Garden of Eden. Man was not satisfied with all the fruits in the garden and needed to take from the one tree forbidden to him. The devil immediately knew what would work best in his quest to deceive man and lure them away from God and good. As time passed, what was considered valuable to man changed. What did not change was the pride and greed that those things deemed "valuable" caused man to feel and the devil's readiness to use that to his advantage. It was once farms and livestock as the necessities of man and life as the precious things that man would covet. As time went on man discovered precious gems and metals and began to covet them. Eventually coins would be made that would serve as currency and furthered the temptations of man. Today, we have seemingly worthless paper that man has declared to be valuable called currency or money. In the United States, we have many nicknames for our currency. Moolah, bucks, cash, and of course the one that leads to the title of this section- the greenback. Whatever name you call it, it is undeniable that money has now become one of the most powerful tools in the devil's arsenal. Now let us dive in head first and explore how the devil uses this "green tea" to tempt humanity to evil.

Money is, of course, relatively new in the history of man. Imagine handing someone a bunch of paper with a portrait of the king and wanting his prized cattle a thousand years ago. The paper itself has no actual value besides the miniscule value of the paper. It is not a product of any precious substance. The currency of today is simply promises by the government that issues them to pay all debts public and private the amount printed on the paper. With the turmoil, upheaval, and corruption that were seen in the "governments" of a thousand years ago no one would consider even selling a lame donkey on a promise to pay. You could trade for the cattle with crops or precious metals- but paper? If you were lucky you would be laughed at and told to leave. If you were unlucky you would be given a thrashing. Luckily for us, those days are long gone. No one questions the value of these pieces of paper now. Food, clothes, and fancy jewelry can all be yours if you have enough of the paper that is deemed money. You could even buy a lame donkey if you really wanted to.

It cannot be questioned that the definition of what is valuable and what is used to conduct business and trade has changed dramatically in the history of man. There is also no question that the devil and his evil have changed accordingly. As crafty and deceptive as ever, the devil now uses our pride and craving for the power that money seems to give man. For the purposes of this section, we will first take a look at the history of money and precious items in the history of man. As we further our look at the history of money, trade, and commerce, it is necessary to look at how the pride of man has been used by the devil to attain his evil desire of pulling man away from God and His good plans for us. Our journey now takes us back in time to see how the quest for money has changed and how it also sparked man's thirst for power. We will finish by looking at the modern world and asking ourselves how powerful the devil's "green tea" is and if man is hopelessly imprisoned by it. It will not give us the answer to our question, but it will get us closer to making our own answer. We will once again go back to the statement "Those who forget the past are doomed to repeat it." As you read this section, ask yourself if we are simply falling for the old tricks of the devil that has already taken down what were thought to be invincible empires.

We will begin our look at historical economies by examining Ancient China. Whereas many of the ancient empires crumbled, China is still around and is now one of the major world powers. As can be expected, China was not always a major world power. The Chinese, however, have been able to maintain "China" as their country and homeland as other empires failed to do so. For our purposes, we will look at the economic reasons that Ancient China would find itself in states of disarray and turmoil. As we look at the major ancient empires, we will see that a strong military was essential. China was no different. We will see that the Chinese dynasties, with the exception of the Mongol invasion, were not toppled because of any invading force. Those dynasties found their downfall in their economic weaknesses. Beginning as an isolationist economy, Ancient

China had a vast country to gain the resources required to make their economy thrive. The problem, as is still the problem even today, was that strong central government proved to be very costly. With its isolationist views and a vast territory, it should come as no surprise that the economies of the various Dynasties in Ancient China were doomed to fall. Looking back with our 20/20 hindsight, Ancient China had all the resources and was so technologically advanced for the times that the various dynasties that ruled it should not have fallen.

There are many reasons why control of Ancient China changed hands so many times. The main reason, it seems, was the reluctance to open its doors to trade with the expanding world. As a whole, the country was leery of foreign trade and did not understand that this trade was necessary to grow its financial state. This was one of the few empires that could have accelerated the Industrial Revolution by a millennium. China's isolationism and rule by the head of whatever dynasty was in charge caused this to be an impossible feat. China would, in fact, stop dominating their European neighbors in GDP per capita as they entered the 19th century. As it entered modern times, the ever singular China adopted a Communist form of government. Whereas the Soviet Union saw its economy and government crumble from a weakening economy, China is now perhaps stronger than ever. An argument could be made that China's growth was hampered by their isolationist past- a thought to keep the riches of their nation for themselves. The days of Chinese isolationism are still with us, but it cannot be denied that they have now found the medium between being an isolated country and being a major power in the world economy.

A jump to later times allows us to consider the empire that was Great Britain and is now the United Kingdom. Great Britain was an empire that at one time had colonies throughout the world that made it both the strongest and the richest nation. From the 17th to 18th centuries, it would be tough to argue that the British Empire was not the strongest nation in the world. American citizens can trace their government roots as part of the colonial force of Great Britain. Having the largest territory in the "New World" simply cemented their place as the economic giant of the time. However, the empire would soon crumble to the point that the United Kingdom sits today. By crumbling I mean just being one of the world's major powers as opposed to THE major power. As a country who just centuries ago was considered the world's greatest power, it will make as an interesting study to see how greed and the quest for ever increasing wealth contributed to the collapse of Great Britain as an empire with territories spanning the globe. As always, we look for the devil to gleefully use his weapon of greed in the events that both led to the rise of the British Empire as well as its "decline".

The "decline" of the British Empire occurred early in the twentieth century. As we will see, the empire which took centuries to fully realize its peak fell from its lofty perch in a matter of decades. It would be very easy to say that the greed for wealth and power in Great Britain and its empire of colonies led to its downturn as a direct result of the government always wanting more. As we will see, however, greed was simply a small cause of their economic downturn and fall from supremacy. The revolutions of the colonies were a hard hit to the Empire, but let us be honest- the cost of maintaining all their colonies was more than what the gains the colonies were providing. Great Britain also held those living in the colonies as "subjects" and not citizens. An argument can be made that most of the citizens of Great Britain came to view the colonies and colonists as an unnecessary expense that was hampering the Empire rather than helping the realm. Despite the cost and internal dislike of the colonies and their subjects, in 1900 the empire of Great Britain controlled about one quarter of territories throughout the world. The devil sat back and watched as Great Britain fell for all his tricks and continued its quest for world domination and the "green tea" it provided. It cannot be denied that the desire for money and power ruled the British Empire in the colonial era.

Going with the theme of this book, one would expect that the greed for wealth would lead to Great Britain's economic downfall. In this case that does not seem to exactly fit. Yes, the widespread territories that it held as well as the class separation between citizens and subjects was a part of the decline, but the next fifty years would be world changing. The two World Wars that were fought in the first half of the twentieth century were a major cause of the economic downfall of Great Britain. In what turned out to be a rather heroic turn, it can be argued that a major cause of the fall of the British Empire was due to the extreme costs of the Wars and their assistance in defeating Hitler's Germany. While the United Kingdom is still one of the world's major economies, it is no longer the world dominator it once was.

For our final look at Ancient economies, we will explore the economy of Ancient Rome. Although the empire crumbled somewhere between the third and fifth centuries A.D., the effect that the Roman Empire has had on man and government can still be seen today. Whereas Ancient China was seen as technologically beyond its time, Ancient Rome could be seen as both an imperial nation and government well before its time. As the Roman Empire expanded its territory, Rome itself was expanding in both a cultural and financial way. The Ancient Roman Empire was perhaps the first Empire that we could consider a world superpower, with the army conquering a majority of the known world. The Roman Empire also included Judea, where Jesus lived and His execution was performed by Romans. With such a rich tradition, infrastructure that other nations would adopt centuries later, and the financial strength that came from its vast empire, it would be difficult to foresee a total collapse of the Roman Empire. Yet, unlike our first two nations, the Roman Empire crumbled and fell and Rome is now the simply the capital of the country of Italy. As we have seen, the dynasties of China and Kings of Great Britain fell from their lofty status but the nations have remained intact. Ancient Rome gives us a good look at how the devil used the trick of his "green tea" to poison the Roman people and their leaders to bring about the fall of an Empire.

Ancient Rome, although it had widespread imperialistic designs, was innovative in the designs and infrastructure of Rome. In fact, the streets of Rome were concrete and had stone roads that were not seen in major cities even one thousand years later. Caligula ordered aqueducts to be built to deliver water into the city. The heart of the innovation of Ancient Rome, however, had to be the legal system that was created for the Empire. By establishing property rights, developing a system for organized trade, as well as offering insurance for long trading voyages, the legal system that Ancient Rome had in place would greatly resemble the systems we see in place today. With the strong Roman army and so many pieces common now in today's world in place, it is difficult to imagine the Roman Empire crumbling away. The previous two Empires that we studied did indeed fall, but the nations of China and England transformed and are still powerful nations today. Rome was enveloped into Italy. Although it is the capital of Italy and still a major city, the fall of the Roman Empire was a complete fall. How did this great Empire completely fail? A strong economy, a strong army, expansive territories- Ancient Rome seemed to have all the necessary components for a nation that would be long lasting. As we look to the fall of the Ancient Roman Empire, let us look at the people and leaders and ask ourselves if the devil used his "green tea" to bring about its destruction.

A common misconception is that the rise of Christianity was a contributing factor to the fall of the Roman Empire. Although Christianity did begin its rise to prominence throughout the Roman Empire, it would be insane to think that an upstart religion could be the reason why an entire empire would fall. As Christianity grew it became an accepted religion in

Rome. The reasons for the fall of the Roman Empire had more to do with the greed of man than anything else. The William Shakespeare classic "Julius Caesar" portrayed an Emperor of Rome who has betrayed and murdered by his friends and enemies in the senate. The event really happened and is an example of how Rome was ruled. It was a place that despite the peace its army had provided to them was full of men who not only possessed but also outwardly acted on the worst qualities of man. Greed and pervasion had more to do with the fall of Rome than the peaceful religion of Christianity could ever have done. As we continue to study the reasons behind the fall of the Roman Empire, we will look at a number of economic and social factors that were contributing factors to its demise. The army, the vast territories, and the advanced infrastructure of Rome could not save it from crumbling away. I chose the Ancient Roman Empire as the last economy because although its reign was two thousand years ago the resemblance to the major powers of today is striking. The influence of the devil on the men of the Roman Empire also mirrors what we see today.

As the Roman economy began to flatten, the emperors took steps to fix it that seem to us now to be done more in panic than through thoughtful reason. The economy of Rome was based upon its superiority in trade and commerce. Technology, besides the infrastructure advances, was not a strong suit of the Roman Empire. With the constant attacks from foreign tribes that Rome constantly warded off and a growing stagnation of Rome's trade market, the Empire soon found itself in a situation where the government was struggling to get their intake to match their outgo. In a time where there were no other countries with which to hold a debt to keep the Empire running smoothly, it was of the utmost importance that Ancient Rome had the funds to pay the many necessary expenses it had. Much like modern economies, Emperor Septimus Severus decided to increase the production of the silver coins used as currency in the Empire and therefore greatly decreasing its value. We now know that producing more currency provides a government with a short term fix, but it also creates a large rate of inflation that will eventually overtake any benefits. In current times, the value of currency is key to the financial strength of a nation's economy, and the inflation rate effects the population and its ability to be contributors to its nation's economic success. The devil's "green tea", in the form of the silver Roman coins, had been brewed and the Romans were not only sipping it but were drinking it down in big gulps.

The Roman Empire saw its downfall completed when Diocletian, a Roman soldier with a rather plain origin, found a way to rise to power and become Emperor of the Empire. As a soldier, Diocletian was able to bring a sense of order to the Empire after a long period of disarray. He doubled the army's size and his rule could be said to mirror the beginnings of Communism in Russia. We cannot say that Diocletian did not do what he thought would save the economy of Rome, but we can say that many of the economic actions he put in place were doomed to fail. He added price controls in an attempt to quell the effects of inflation, which simply led producers to sell their products in trade. He also centralized the production of all resources under the Roman Empire's control. This caused the government to have exceedingly high costs, which of course was followed by high taxes on the Roman people. It got to the point where land owners would choose to abandon their properties as opposed to paying the high tax. Diocletian went as far as enslaving the Roman people by forcing the work of skilled laborers and demanding men to follow the professions of their fathers. As he frustratingly watched all his actions fail, Diocletian did something that the Emperors before him did not. In an Empire where the emperor always stayed in power until their death- either by natural causes or by murder- Diocletian retired as emperor and left Ancient Rome in a situation where recovery was impossible.

We have seen the decline of empires that were expected to live on throughout time and studied what brought about either their decline or in Rome's case total collapse. In our studies, what pops out is the difficulty that man has when given everything one could want. It is quite obvious then that the devil's great weapon of greed has historically been a downfall of man. From wanting the fruit of the forbidden tree to the quests for world domination that occurred soon after the discovery of the "New World", enough has never truly been enough for man. As the devil lured us to eat from the Forbidden Tree, so too has he lured us into centuries of bloodshed, slavery, and outright thievery to help us attain what we thought we needed- MORE.   We have seen this in today's world as the greed of man has very recently thrown the world economy into disarray.   History has taught us that when nations find themselves in a situation where money becomes an issue bloodshed soon follows.   Many Americans today think of the wars we have fought and continue to fight in the Middle East are simply battles to obtain the oil those countries have and the money that the usage of oil provides.   The dependence on oil, the devil's "black tea", is the focus of our next section.   For now, we will close our study of the usage of the devil's "green tea" in the country whose currency's color and its nickname of greenback gave us the title for this section.   I think it safe to say our study of the economies of the past is finished, so let us now examine just how the devil is using our hunger for wealth in modern times.   Let us look at the economy of the United States of America, whose rise from British colony to world superpower is unsurpassed.

The country that we know as the USA was formed when thirteen British Colonies in the New World declared their independence and won a war for their freedom. The new country, separated from any enemies to their freedom by the massive Atlantic Ocean, was able to grow and thrive. The Louisiana Purchase gave the new country a territory that greatly increased its size. The young United States had left its infancy and with the expanse that is the North American continent the possibilities seemed endless. I would like to say that the expansion of the United States continued with peaceful purchases of land but we know that is not the case. In school I learned the American theory of Manifest Destiny, which basically says our way is better than yours and we are going to expand and grow as much as we want. It seemed innocent enough to me as a school child, but as I grew I learned the extent that America was willing to go to make the country span from coast to coast. Sadly enough, it is the true "owners" of the country that found themselves in the crosshairs. The Native Americans did not keep population records but history shows us that genocide was committed in the Westward expansion. A common argument of the time was that we were given the country by God, and God would want us to spread His word and democracy. The devil must have laughed at this. He knew the real reason why America was expanding. It was not providence. It was not to spread democracy. The devil had planted the seeds of greed in man long ago. It was just a matter of time before his "green tea" expanded to the North American continent.

As in every country, Americans tend to focus on the great achievements of their homeland and turn a blind eye to its downsides. We laud Abraham Lincoln for his Emancipation Proclamation that freed the slaves but the evils of the American slave culture are not spoken of nearly enough. Can it be denied that the early American economy depended on taking away the basic rights of their fellow man and forcing them into unpaid and unappreciated work? That would probably cause an argument that would take this book in a direction it should not go, but please think of how the devil had always been at work playing on the greed of man and always making sure our cup of green tea has just enough to make us desire more. As the young country grew into a world power, it's craving for the "green tea" exploded to unseen levels. We have looked at economies of the past, but now we jump to recent times and will explore the recent world economic downturn and near collapse that began in 2008. While there are many factors that led to this situation, we will look focus our at the mortgage industry and how the greed of man not only caused a downturn in the housing market but also destroyed the lives and financial security of millions.

As I was growing up, I did not know what they did but I was always intrigued when I heard the newscasts talk about Fannie and Freddy. They were usually talked about in small snippets of the financial part of the news right before sports. As time went on and my education grew, I eventually learned that Fannie Mae and Freddie Mac were private companies supported by the U.S. government and both entities were in the business of issuing mortgages and home loans. The heart of the American dream of homeownership often came to fruition with a loan from Freddie or Fannie. For generations, Fannie Mae and Freddie Mac acted as a helper to the American people in attaining that dream. As Bill Clinton brought the American economy out of the deficit and downturn of the early 1990s, he turned towards American home ownership as a priority. Perhaps a blindly noble effort, Clinton sought the assistance of private enterprises to achieve his goal of making home ownership more affordable to the American people and getting the rate of home ownership to seventy percent of American citizens. At that point in time, home ownership in America was in the 60% range, so jumping to 70% was not exactly a radical idea. Opening up the mortgage markets to so many different private entities was. Looking back, we can see how the devil must have had a sly smile as this took place. Man made it way too easy for him to plant his temptations and lure him away from God. The kettle began to whistle. A fresh brew of green tea was ready for humans to devour and fight over.

The list of guilty of parties in the collapse of the home finance market and downturn in the housing market is as long as a career criminal's rap sheet. The names included people in the highest government positions, those at the top of major financial institutions, and you and me. While most in the American public are content with cursing big business and seemingly invisible mortgage companies for the collapse, few- if any- are willing to turn their eyes upon themselves. I will be honest and admit that I almost became a part of the problem. When I was with my ex-wife I decided that we should buy a home- a condo listed for $349,000 located in a good school district in the upper suburbs of New York City. Our credit was not the best, and my ex-wife questioned if we could pull it off. I said something that must have been said by many before the crises hit- "Why not? Everyone is buying a house these days." I look back on that with shame. Especially since the mortgage we had been approved for was at 8.25% and in two years would have jumped to almost 11%. You don't have to rub your eyes- it really was eight and a quarter percent. And I really thought we could pull it off. This all occurred right as the government started to realize that perhaps the mortgage industry had gotten out of control. The sellers stalled long enough- not wanting to drop to the price I was willing to pay- that the new government policies meant we no longer qualified for the mortgage. As the economy crashed a year later, it finally hit me. Those stories of defaults, the stories of people losing their homes- that very well could have been me. The green tea of the devil may have hit me in other ways, but I was somehow saved from the housing crash.

Although the mortgage crisis saw many corporate hands stirring the pot of devilish green tea, Countrywide is the company that took a lot- if not most- of the blame. Countrywide Financial was a home finance company whose "creative" mortgage options played on the greed of people who honestly (or not) thought that buying a home was within their reach. I say "was" because the company known as Countrywide Financial eventually fell under the weight of the massive bad loans that it had issued. The "predatory lending" practices of Countrywide and numerous smaller mortgage originators fueled the fire of the impending crash. Although it was not the collapse that would later be seen in Lehman Brothers, it is undeniable that the acquisition of Countrywide by Bank of America prevented its complete and utter failure. The acquisition occurred right before we realized the extent of the problem. Although, it was sold off before it collapsed, Countrywide was the first domino to fall in the impending crash. Bank of America became the nation's largest holder of mortgages and the CEO of Countrywide walked away from the mess with $67 million as a parting "thank you" from Countrywide. Each side's greed was satisfied, but the worst for the industry and economy was yet to come. The Great Depression of 2008 may have been averted by programs of the U.S. government or the depression may be yet to come. The one thing that we can say for sure is that the devil must have brewed this latest batch of his green tea especially strong.

In the last few years we have seen the total collapse of the financial giant Lehman Brothers, as well as the forced takeovers of such companies as Bear Stearns and Washington Mutual. We have also seen the "too big to fail" policy which protected the major banks of the United States from falling into bankruptcy and collapse. The big banks were all given $25 billion dollar loans as part of the TARP program to ensure their solvency. While the banks from weakest to strongest remained solvent and eventually were able to turn their financial tide from the red and back into the black, the effects of the financial crises that began in 2008 are still with us today. The "bail-out" of the American banking system succeeded since every major U.S. bank is still operational and turning a profit. Wachovia was sold to Wells Fargo and although the public believed it was because of Wachovia's failed business those in control of the two entities attempted to explain the transaction as just a simple business decision. The argument that was being made to the public was that if the huge U.S. banks were allowed to fail the effect on the overall economy of the nation would be devastating. That argument may very well have been a sound one. We will never know if the markets and economy could have survived if Citibank was allowed to fall. What we do know is that these companies and the people who were (or still are) running them drank copious amounts of the devil's green tea and when the crows came to roost they were saved by the government. It was, perhaps, one of those situations where something had to be done to protect the welfare of the citizens of the country. The everyday average Joe does not look at things like that. Everyday people see major corporations "given" billions to help them as they clean up their mistakes and ask- "Well, where's my bailout?"

The American public was now in a state of both denial and anger. As 2008 continued they found themselves either struggling to make their mortgage payment or worse falling into delinquency and foreclosure. As we watched that occurring who could question those people who were losing their homes as they questioned, "Where is my bailout?" We watched mothers cry as they told their story on the news and wondered along with them just where their children would go. It was impossible not to gain sympathy and demand an answer to the question of where was the help for these poor people. We have spent a long time talking about the greed of man and their abnormal lust for more and more. No one can question that this is a strategy of the devil that he has played on throughout the time of man. Hey Adam! Hey Eve! The only reason God does not want you to eat the fruit from that tree is that He knows you will become gods if you do so. Jesus, if you truly are the Son of God come with me and we will rule the world. Adolph, you know your people are the best of the best. It is time for you to cleanse the world of the inferior people and take your position as the leader of the master race. In those three examples, we again see how man so easily falls while the devil has no power over God. Following those examples one might be lured to say the question is already answered. The devil has an extreme power over man but no power over God. We will explore those points and theological points on why the devil still feels he was a chance to conquer God and regain his place in Heaven. For now, however, we will continue our study on how the devil tempts and deceives human beings to move away from the will of God.

Our study of the devil's "green tea" has shown us that man has an extreme weakness for the power afforded to him by whatever is deemed as "wealth" in society. While we cannot deny this weakness, man has not completely fallen in love with the greed and power that wealth tends to give them- if even only fleetingly. Man still has that place in his soul that loves God, fears His disappointment, and has care for his fellow man. The devil, of course, was not finished with his tricks and deception. The green tea was indeed potent and worked well to tempt humans away from the grace of God. Was it enough? Was anything ever enough for the devil? God's earth, of course, provided man with all he could ever need. The devil knows this and still has some tricks up his sleeve. As we continue our study on the tricks and deception of the devil, let us move to his "black tea". Held in his back pocket for so long, once the twentieth century was upon us it became ready to unleash on the world. Let us now move on, and study how the devil has used crude oil to further man's greed and move him away from the will of God and of good.

IV

We must always remember that the devil is an angel whose pride and deceptive nature led him away from the grace of God. The devil actually declared war upon God and after a fierce battle was defeated. The devil was, of course, cast out of Heaven never to return. Thrown to a desolate pit of despair, the devil wasted no time plotting his revenge. His best, if not only hope, was to get man to turn his back on God. His first interaction with man in the Garden showed him that this was possible. It must have seemed not only possible but laughably simple. The devil may have been cast out of Heaven, but he had free rein on the Earth. He saw the black liquid held within the earth. Although there was no use for the grotesque substance yet, the devil knew the potential that it held. Man, thanks to his nudging, would eventually grow to the point where they understood the power of this liquid. As the technology of man increased, so did their desire for oil. It was quite an amazing thing to see how the world became dependent on crude oil so quickly. The devil, of course, was there every step of the way to use this "black tea" to his advantage.

The craze for oil is a new occurrence in the history of man. There simply was no need for the black, gooey stuff in early history. It was not useful to man and therefore undesirable. Technology, however, boomed in the twentieth century. Henry Ford developed the assembly line which made automobiles an affordable option for Americans. As crude oil was the life blood of the fuel that made automobiles run, it instantly became a commodity that man desired. The technology of man, the wealth of man, and his dependence on that gunky stuff would explode throughout the 1900s. Crude oil would also prove to have a number of uses that simply increased its value. This has been particularly true in the past forty years, where the price of crude oil has been volatile varying from under $10 a barrel to a recent max of over $145 a barrel. With the world consuming nearly 90 million barrels of oil and fuel a day, it is easy to see that the money involved in crude oil is astronomical. The emergence and our dependence on oil has set the stage perfectly for the devil. In it, he has found a way to use all of man's weaknesses together to set up his ultimate plan for the downfall of God's chosen people.

Everything we use today seems to have a need for oil. We drive in our gasoline powered cars. We sit in comfort, even in winter, because of the oil furnaces that provide us heat. Plastic, fertilizer, and synthetic rubber are all products that we derive from crude oil. The needs of man have seemed to move away from the necessities that man had once desired. In the countries deemed to be first world there seems to be little concern about a shortage of food. There is little, if any, concern of how well the harvest will be this season. The world, in its never ending cycle of change, has moved away from coveting the necessities of life to desiring luxurious things. In today's world the things that are coveted the most- while we consider them to be necessities- are truly nothing more than needless excess. The devil's job was easy when it came to his black tea. In it, he found something that could be used to attack all the vices of man. Greed, the desire for power, and envy can all be seen in human's reaction towards oil and the things that it "provides" to man. As we review the history of crude oil and its hold on man, we will look at some of the major players who have brought us to the point we are in today. They are without a doubt human, but see if you can find the influences of the devil in these figures. I have no doubt you will.

I grew up in the Bronx, a borough of New York City. It was only a thirty minute ride on the six train to Midtown Manhattan. After that it was a quick hop over to Rockefeller Center to see the majestic Christmas tree they put up every year. As a youngster, I never considered where the name "Rockefeller Center" came from. I was too enthralled with the tree and the glorious nature which is New York City. Later on in life, I learned that the name came from John D. Rockefeller. A great philanthropist later in life, Rockefeller amassed his great fortune in the oil business. He would later be called the creator of the American oil industry. As Rockefeller has had such an influence on American culture and its oil dependency, it makes sense for us to start our study with him. Standard Oil. Esso. The beginning of the corruption and deceit between oil companies and governments. In America, that began with John D. Rockefeller, whose oil exploits proved him to be a selfish profiteer who aimed to dominate the American oil market. It is more than likely that the American dependence on oil and the greed it causes would have happened with or without Rockefeller. It is nevertheless a fact that his influence directed the future of the oil industry.

Rockefeller chose to run his Standard Oil with an iron fist, looking to destroy any and all competition in his way. Even as his Standard Oil dominated almost all of the American oil supplies, Rockefeller was known to bemoan the effects of competition on his business. The fact the he was becoming one of the richest men in the world did not stop Rockefeller from wanting more. Truth be told, Rockefeller would not be happy until he controlled the entire American oil market. Standard Oil would, however, come under fire from the U.S. government because of the monopolistic hold it had on the oil industry. Standard Oil would be broken up, and the companies formed in its wake would make up many components of the American oil industry we know of today. Rockefeller was given major shareholder positions in all the companies, so his status as the richest man in American and perhaps the world remained solid. Rockefeller, though, was different from the oil moguls of today. He set strict standards for Standard Oil- set in place to avoid both financial and technical catastrophes. Despite being nailed by the Supreme Court for the monopoly of Standard Oil, Rockefeller demanded his companies play within the rules. After his retirement, Rockefeller moved on to philanthropy and created many trusts to fund the public good.

During his time running Standard Oil, Rockefeller was often vilified by the press and in turn by the American people. The plan of the devil was in full effect. Rockefeller could be seen as fueled by greed and a desire for power. People were struck by jealousy and envy over his wealth and success. While the riches and power that Rockefeller enjoyed were tremendous (as well as his philanthropy later in life), the greed of the oil industry would explode to the dangerous point it is at today after his retirement and death. Countries, oligarchies, big business, and maybe your relative who has that cushy job on Wall Street all have their hands swirling the "black tea". The devil's plan, it seemed, was all going according to plan. Sure, an additional nudge is occasionally needed here or there, but everything that was needed to tempt and lure man was in place. As the twentieth century continued, oil's hold on man continued to tighten. It became the epicenter for all of man's evil traits. Rockefeller's Standard Oil was king in the late 19th to early 20th centuries. As man's dependence on oil grew, so did the greed caused by every facet of the oil industry. It began to be a worldwide desire, almost every inch of the planet became dependent on the gooey black liquid. We will now look at the last forty years of the oil era, as it is perhaps the biggest reason that the people today are seriously questioning whether the devil is winning. We will begin with the emergence of Middle Eastern oil and look at all the evils that have been caused by oil.

The Organization of Petroleum Exporting Companies (OPEC) is a group formed from the oil producing countries of the Middle East. Before the foundation of OPEC in 1960, the major oil companies set the price they would pay for crude oil. A barrel of oil cost an amount that would seem unfathomable to anyone today- under $4 a barrel. The so called Seven Sisters controlled almost all of the world's reserves of oil and did not negotiate with Middle Eastern countries on the price they would pay for crude oil. They set the price they would pay and there was nothing the Middle Eastern countries could do about it.

OPEC was formed to stop the price fixing and increase the price paid to the countries in the Middle East. The efforts of OPEC were largely a failure until the Shah of Iran and Muammar Gaddafi decided to nationalize their countries' oil industries. With the Middle Eastern Oil of two major producers now in the hands of dictators, the days of low cost oil would quickly come to an end.

The greed that oil would cause was already set in place. Rockefeller in his quest to monopolize the American oil industry and the Seven Sisters use of price fixing to ensure big profits are just examples of how far humans would go to squeeze as much money from oil as they could. The emergence of OPEC and the vast amounts of oil in the Middle East created a whole new battlefield for the devil to play in. The greed, of course, never left. If anything, we can say that the power of greed exploded to unseen levels after OPEC exercised its domination over world oil markets. While that greed exploded into a worldwide phenomenon, the devil had just begun to use all the evils that his black tea held. Greed, although its hold on man is extremely powerful, was just not enough for the devil. The power of his black tea was just starting to be realized and the devil would sit back as greed was joined by jealousy, anger, and violence. Some might say that mankind did not have a chance. I say that man always has a chance to reject the lures of the devil. That being said, history has shown us that man is all too often weaker than the temptations of the devil. As we continue our study of the effects of oil on man, we will now look at how the oil industry has brought out the very worst of mankind.

As the Seven Sisters and their price fixing cartel collapsed, OPEC was now allowed to set their own price for oil. Traders also began to trade oil as a commodity. The mix of the two would create a situation where the greed of man would be pushed to the limit and the world would become hostage to oil. The "black tea" would cause wars, economic downturns, and environmental destruction. It is impossible that man did not see this as it was happening, but it is still occurring to this very day. As the increased price of oil built luxurious palaces in the Middle East it also built luxurious mansions here in America. There are many facets to the evils that were caused by man's dependence on oil. We will begin by looking at the culture that caused oil to jump from its meager early price to the insane price of over $140 dollars a barrel in 2008. It is a story of greed. It is a story of jealousy. It is a story of the worst of mankind. It is a story that the devil is proud to be a contributing element. The story of speculation, greed, and profiteering is a good enough place to begin our look at the current state of the oil industry and the effect that it has had on humanity. Greed, it seems, is usually the precursor to further evils and it is no different here.

The trading of oil as a commodity was a rare occurrence until the 1970s. Until then, the Seven Sisters had a death grip on OPEC and the price of oil. The rise of Gaddafi in Libya as well as the monarchy of the Shah of Iran helped lead the world into a new age of the oil industry. In this new age, which we are still in, the world has become totally dependent on crude oil. With this dependence, the devil is able to easily use our "needs" to further his deception and lead man away from God's will. The beginning was very small, with the trade of oil companies' excess oil in Rotterdam. Although it began on a small scale, eventually the trading and speculation done at this port would become the price maker for oil. The Arab countries loved that the fixed price of the Seven Sisters was now a thing of the past. Traders saw an unregulated marketplace where their greed could be fed with very little interference. The stage was now set for the devil's largest attack on mankind. Three key elements were essential in this attack- man's need for oil, the controlling countries' knowledge that they held the key that kept the world going, and of course the greed that seems to be inherent in man. These elements quickly combined and soon became a powder keg. A powder keg that has threatened to explode the last forty years, and who knows what or who will be left in its wake if it does.

In our quick look at the beginnings of the oil industry, we saw how it was run by greed for money and the power it provided the major oil companies and countries that produced the valuable liquid. Amazingly enough, the cartels of the oil companies and oil producing countries, while not really concealing their greed, led the oil industry in a somewhat peaceful fashion until the 1970s. It was then that the selfishness and greed of man really started to raise its ugly head. Dictators, governments, traders, and terrorists would all have a hand in directing the route that the oil industry was about to take. The oil that we now use is the product of hundreds of millions of years of decay and the fossils left behind. As a result, it is a non-renewable energy source that is limited in its supply. Mankind, as we well know, reverts back to their infant state when they are told they cannot have something. Unfortunately, when mankind has a temper tantrum as adults the repercussions are much bigger. The past forty years have shown us just how bad the tantrums over oil can be. Lives have been lost, countries have seen their infrastructure crushed, and "everyday people" have seen their ability to continue their everyday lives compromised. This book started with the attacks of 9/11. Oil was never mentioned as a reason for the attacks, but one would have to be very gullible to believe that it had no role in those attacks. Perhaps it was not a given reason, but it cannot be denied that the greed caused by the oil of the Middle East was indeed a reason. To begin our look at the greed and subsequent violence caused by oil, let us go to 1973 and an attack by Arab countries looking to invade Israel.

The war, fought in October of 1973, saw the oil rich state of Syria and Egypt attack Israel. As with every conflict these days, there was no clear reason for the attack. The world was in the clenches of the cold war, so the United States and the Soviet Union took up opposing sides in the conflict. As Israel and the United States were long standing allies, it obviously supported the Israelis while Communist Russia supported the Arab states. The war only lasted a little over two weeks, but the repercussions were solid and long lasting. For the first time, the Arab world was able to not only threaten but also successfully attack Israel and gain some spoils when the cease fire was announced. The Arab states now knew that in the midst of the Cold War they could rely on Soviet assistance. The war, while it seems on a small stage now, had repercussions that were rather grand in scale and that we still feel to this day. Our allegiance to Israel formed the United States as the enemy in the minds of the Arab states. The conflict also showed the world that the oil producing Arab states could no longer be pushed around.

The conflict, as all conflicts do, had serious ramifications for the countries involved. Lives were lost, although with such a quick conflict they were not monumental. Thousands of miles away and far from the gunfire the conflict had caused a new evil to emerge. The Middle Eastern oil producers declared an embargo on shipments of oil to the Western world. The lines at gas stations in America just proved to us how dependent the country had become on oil. It also showed that the American people were using an extreme amount of crude oil. While the amount of oil produced on American soil was still substantial, the lack of Middle Eastern oil proved that as a country we were now relying on the resources from other countries to thrive. Although the everyday American was dependent on oil for their everyday lives, there become a small group of people spread throughout the world that would use the turmoil, violence, and oil embargoes that occurred to make themselves rich. As time went on and the trade of oil became a part of the mainstream, the greed for the profits that the devil's "black tea" offered seemed almost as easy as plucking that fruit from the Garden of Eden.

Man has shown throughout history that there is very little that will deter his greed once it has taken grip. The fighting in 1973 was no different. Money, as it always has been, was the target. The only change was that man would now be using oil to pacify his greed. The attack by the Arab states was a long rumored possibility, and if it came to pass the profits an oil trader might see would be monumental. One such trader saw the possibilities, made secret deals with the Shah of Iran, and bought up Iranian oil for storage in the case of an upcoming oil supply disturbance. Although his company sold off the oil before any conflict, the stage was now set. Corrupt government officials and greedy individuals with the cash to bribe said corrupt officials is never a good thing. The price of oil would continue to climb and despite efforts by the West, the stabilization of prices would be constantly threatened by both world events and speculators in the trading market. As we know, the world was bound to continue along the chaotic path that had been begun by the advances that made oil a necessity. To compound matters, the pro-west Shah of Iran was thrown out of power and replaced by a Muslim fundamentalist government. Greed and power, although they remained strong influences, were now joined by a new religious angle.

The 1980s, while still in the vise like grip of oil, is remembered more for the greed and major political events that dominated the decade. The stock market boomed and Reagan demanded that Gorbachev take down the Berlin Wall. Oil, as well, had a prominent effect on the world during the decade. As opposed to the previous decade it was not shortages or high prices that were affecting the people and the world- it was the opposite. During the eighties, we here in America watched as the Soviet Union started to collapse and mourned as a space shuttle exploded soon after liftoff. At the same time the world found itself with a greater supply of oil than the world demanded. The price of oil, following the rules of economics, dropped from its highs to lows back around $10 a barrel. As the NYSE boomed and our enemy the Soviet Union began to crumble, Americans paid little attention to what the low price of oil was doing to countries whose economies relied on the money that oil provided. Those who were looking intently at the situation may have realized that without an excess of oil profits the Soviet Union's economy started to break down. Some may have glanced at newspaper articles reporting that the low prices of oil caused some countries to fall into bankruptcy. The public, or at least the American public, were focused solely on the imminent collapse of the Soviet Union and our "win" in the Cold War. Those who were involved in the oil trade, however, viewed the events occurring in society with a different glance. They were always looking for ways to feed their insatiable greed and regardless of the price oil always filled their desires.

The eighties found the price of oil once again leaving the hands of its producing states. Early in the decade, the price of oil moved to being controlled by "speculators" in the futures market. As this scenario unfolded, it was hated by both the major oil companies and by OPEC. This new way of pricing for crude oil, however, was here to stay. Aggressive and knowledgeable traders were able to take positions in crude oil and, despite the price, make huge profits from their trades. Options in the delivery of oil were also introduced. Now, the profits from the trade of oil were not limited to oil companies and large investment firms, but were open to the public. Now that everyone had the option to be in the big oil game, it was simply a matter of time before the greed of man made it explode out of control. That, however, was still years away. It was still the eighties, where cash was king and the black tea of the devil was as willing as ever to provide man with the money to fill his greed. Even as the price of oil crashed from over $30 a barrel to under $10 a barrel, man found a way to profit. The advent of the futures trade of oil meant that companies could hold large paper contracts on the delivery of oil. They were able to control prices with the large holdings of oil options, and often traders were happy with a simple penny a barrel profits. With the stage pretty much set for the future, we will now jump forward and look at some of the events that led up to the crude oil highs in 2008 and how the greed of man brought the price of oil to amounts never even imagined just years before the peak was reached.

The world's demand for oil continued to increase, and accordingly the greed of man followed suit. In 1990, Saddam Hussein, dictator of Iraq, invaded Kuwait. They were both oil rich countries, the difference being Kuwait was friendlier to the Western world than the Iraqi dictatorship was. U.S. President George Bush Sr. declared there would be a military strike to regain Kuwait's freedom. To the American people, it was portrayed as America defending freedom in the world. Hussein was portrayed as the epitome of evil who must be stopped. Whitney Houston sang perhaps the best national anthem ever given at a sporting event. For the American public, national pride was high. They looked to their President with pride as he stood firm against those who would challenge democracy. The American public was happy, but those involved in the American oil business were not particularly pleased with the President's quick response to the invasion of Kuwait. Bush Sr., a Texas Republican, would let the oil fields in Texas sit abandoned while he sent the armed forces of the United States military to a foreign land to protect America's interests in the 1.5 million barrel daily supply of Kuwait's crude oil. The American oil producers in Texas were outraged. While their country was willing to fight for a foreign country, their interests were largely ignored. Although not exactly in vogue after freeing Kuwait from the invading Iraqis, this would perhaps be the first time that the money gained from using military force to obtain oil rights was termed "blood for oil". As the devil sat back and watched mankind fall face first into his trap he knew that this was not the end. The devil was not finished and the evil man would go to collecting both the oil and money that it produced were just beginning to reach levels higher than ever imagined.

At the start of this book, the terrifying events of September 11, 2001 were chronicled in detail. While we explained the act of terrorism and the horror delivered by those four planes, the aftereffects of that day also deserve our attention. That day has become known as the day that forever changed the world. One thing we found out for sure is that the world would never again have that blanket of safety to hide in. If terrorists were able to infiltrate the mighty United States and successfully attack the symbols of America's wealth and its military strength, what would keep them from staging attacks in any other democratic country? The new normal I talked about in the opening is a world in which people live in a state that contains an equal measure of fear and apprehension.

Wall Street, the base of the American stock exchange, stands one mile from the World Trade Center site. Although it was spared any major physical damage, even the ruthless realm of the NYSE's trading floor took an emotional hit. Various investment firms had offices in or near the WTC site and hundreds of people whose job revolved around Wall Street were no longer with us. Besides the loss of life, Wall Street also had to deal with the fear of the whether the attacks were done. With two enormous symbols of America's wealth now gone, what was stopping the terrorists from attacking Wall Street? The days following 9/11 gave us no answer to that question. Although we cannot still definitively say that the financial locations of lower Manhattan are not in the crosshairs, Wall Street reopened for business just one week after the tragedy.

As America tried its best to get back to business, Wall Street started with the apprehension that the events of the previous week deserved. People were fearful of what the future might hold and the selloff in that opening week was immense. U.S. stocks took over a trillion dollars in losses. On September 10th, 2001, the price for a barrel of crude oil was below $30. It did not rise considerably after the markets reopened, as the threat of an impending recession would mean that the demand for oil would not be as high. As America started to get used to the new post 9/11 normal, the recession ended and the trade of oil would enter a period that even the most optimistic of traders, oil companies, or dictators could not imagine. The price of crude oil which sat below $30 a barrel was about to begin its journey to almost $150 a barrel. As we have already covered, the greed caused by oil was seen in every aspect of mankind. Companies, governments, and the average every day person were all affected in some way by the oil boom. For me, the first gas station shock came after Hurricane Katrina devastated New Orleans and greatly damaged the oil that was supplied from the Gulf of Mexico. I had watched, with very little care and concern, as gas rose from the mid one dollar range to around the mid two dollar range the previous ten years. For some reason this jump hit me. Perhaps it was the images of how badly New Orleans had been hit. Perhaps it was the obvious price gouging that was going on. Little did I know, this may have simply have been a harbinger of what was to come. The days of $2.30 a gallon for gas were coming to an end- perhaps never to return. The devil, ever wily, was about to mix his ever strong green tea with that of his increasingly potent black tea and unleash it upon man.

After the disaster of Hurricane Katrina, the price of gasoline came back down and the cost of a barrel of oil at the end of 2005 settled at around $60 a barrel. The disaster showed the devil that his plan would work. While upset with the price gouging seen at many gas stations people, myself included, continued to travel and go to the pump and pay what we thought were outrageous prices. The black tea had made us completely dependent on crude oil. The second stage of the devil's plan was about to explode on the world. As we have already discussed, the price of oil became something not necessarily decided by the economic law of supply and demand. Speculation in the world stock markets would lead the way to the price of oil jumping nearly 150% as it made its way to its highs in 2008. The mix of the black tea and the green tea became an irresistible combination to people. Oil, although a recent addiction to the world, was without a doubt the most powerful deception that the devil had used. Through his black tea the devil was able to gain control over not only man's desire for power (to become like gods) but also to feed man's greed for wealth. The oil craze that occurred culminated in 2008 and has only dampened slightly. It is still considered a major reason why people ask if the devil is now winning. Gas prices now sit at the post-Katrina gouge highs. Mortgages are near impossible to get, the American Dream of home ownership seems impossible to attain, and there seems to be less and less of a Middle Class these days. As I was writing the last few sentences, it occurred to me that the fact that people are asking the question more and more these days should come as very little surprise.

At this point, my research on the two "teas" that the devil uses to tempt man away from the will of God is complete. I know that the two topics we explored could each fill a book (as well as many other forms of temptation the devil uses), but these two subjects were enough to point out the major reasons why we now ask if the devil has taken the upper hand. As this book reaches its end, I will start by looking at the theological answers to the question, and finish with my own. As I stated earlier, it is impossible for us as humans to come up with a definitive answer to the question "Is the devil winning?" Man thinking that we ever could might be considered slightly akin to Adam and Eve eating the fruit from the tree. We must understand this and as we come up with our own answers to the question we must admit and fully embrace that it is only our own thoughts of the matter. I am sure that if you have continued reading to this point you most likely have your own answer prepared. If anything, the words you have read thus far have led you to say, "Of course the devil is winning!" Hold your horses (or your lame donkey if you were foolish enough to buy one). The devil's cards have been flipped over and he has shown a hand of four jacks. For all those who are not poker aficionados, the devil's four of a kind seems an impossible hand to beat. The devil, with his ever failing pride, is one to count his chickens before they hatch. In this case he is counting his chips before God flips over his cards. In the final two sections we will explore the theological answers as well as my own personal answer to the question and try to discern just what cards God is holding.

V

When looking at theological sources one thing is always a constant- God wins and the devil loses. Why, then, are we increasingly asking whether the devil is taking the upper hand over God? More than half of the world's population are followers of either the Muslim or Christian faiths. The holy books of the two faiths both come to the same conclusion- God conquers and the devil falls in ruin. Each book has their own unique story on how the end of days will turn out but each finishes by giving great hope to the faithful. Followers of the world's two major religions believe that the words of the Qur'an and the Bible are written by the hands of man but were given by either the prophecies Allah gave to the Prophet Mohammed or by the divine inspiration that God gave to the writers of the Bible. Looking at it this way, one can say that those asking the question are committing a sin just by considering whether something that is written in these holy works is not true. Is our free will leading us down a path of sin? Is the devil leading us down that path? In this section we will explore the theological texts and their response to the question. It should come as no surprise that the answer to our question is a resounding "NO!" from the theological works that we will look at. I can hear the arguments now- I read this entire book and your answer is just going to something I could have read in the Bible? Relax. If you have been faithfully reading you know that this is not the end, and I will not take the "easy" out of saying this is what the bible says and you better believe it. This book was never about questioning anyone's faith nor will it begin to do so. The question the book asks, though, is deep in theological tones. While we have briefly touched on the theological views of the devil in the second section of this book, I think I would fail in my attempt to answer the question if I did not take a deeper look into the theological answers to our question.

In the Islamic faith, while still believing in Iblis as a fallen angel whose mission is to lure man away from Allah's straight path, the End of Days story told in the Qur'an is rather troublesome for the question of the book. As was seen in the second section, there is no struggle for power between Allah and Iblis when that time comes. As opposed to the common view of the Christian world, Iblis upholds his agreement with Allah and goes to the abyss and fires of Hell without a fight. When those that were fooled and followed his evil ways come to him for help, Iblis basically says "Sucks to be you" and watches as every mortal that has fallen for his tricks and whispers is sent to hell. If we were looking at the Qur'an as a piece of modern literature, or as a movie script, we would probably say this is a terrible ending or close the book feeling unsatisfied. The Qur'an, however, is not just a simple book written for the entertainment of the masses. It is a book that leads the followers of Allah to follow his straight path to salvation and explains how Iblis will attempt to fool them with his whispers to get man to stray from what should be the ultimate goal of salvation. Although Iblis and his ultimate end will come with barely a whimper, the question the book asks is still a valid one. The downfall of Iblis in the Qur'an is without a doubt much different than that of Satan in the Bible. The one constant in both religious books is that man is drawn away from God's graces by an evil fallen angel. While there should be no question about the outcome, there is still a question as to whether Iblis or Satan, is winning. The goal of eternal salvation, which should be man's ultimate goal, has perhaps become even more difficult to reach with the assistance of the devil.

When thinking of salvation as our ultimate destination, I will use a modern example to explain Iblis's evil works and their effects on man reaching the ultimate prize of salvation. Picture the entrance to salvation as the line outside of a very exclusive nightclub, with all of man craving entrance to the everlasting good that is within the gates. Those who have been able to stay on Allah's straight path are escorted to the front of the line and allowed to enter paradise. What happens to those who were unable to stay on Allah's straight path is crushing. The glorious lights are replaced by a rather dim haze. The gates which stood majestic are now gone. In its place, a massive gap in the earth has formed. As the fallen reach the front, they see Iblis standing by the edge of the abyss. The fallen beg him for mercy. The fallen beg him for an answer. Iblis has nothing for these fallen souls and watches as they are thrown into the abyss of Hell. The devil has never had any concern for the plight of man and is not about to start caring. The question of the devil winning may take on different qualities in the religious works of

Islam and Christianity- but one thing does remain the same. Man is easily fooled by the whispers and temptations given to him by the fallen angel of God. In the Qur'an this leads to the downfall of those who stray and they are doomed to hell. While many consider the question of "Is the Devil Winning?" a question of the devil versus God, the Islamic faith does not even consider that question.

The question in the Islamic faith is more of an internal question that the followers of Allah need to ask themselves every day. The Qur'an spells out quite clearly what will happen to the devil as our mortal lives on Earth cease to exist. He has already accepted his fate as being thrown into hell. The question is for the souls of man. Who will join Iblis in Hell? In my view, that is what the Qur'an is trying to prevent. Allah loves man and wishes them all to follow his straight path and join him in paradise. Allah, in His glory, only wishes that the good followers who have stayed true to his straight path join him in paradise. Entrance into paradise is the gift the Allah has offered to man. While Allah may be disappointed by the fall of so many, the all-powerful and knowing Allah accepts that man may fail in the simple task He has given to them. In the end, it could be three hundred or three billion that join Allah in paradise. The power of Allah will never be challenged and He will accept those who have faithfully followed Him. As will be further shown in the Christian Bible, the story has a happy ending. Iblis is sent to hell with those foolish enough to follow him and those who have remained loyal to Allah will be welcomed with open arms and join Allah in Paradise.

As we shift to the Christian Bible, we must first look at the differences between the Bible and the Qur'an and their views of the devil. There can be no doubt that the differences in the views of the two religious works are in stark contrast. In the Qur'an, Iblis refuses to follow Allah's orders and is cast out of paradise. In the Bible, however, the devil is polluted by his pride even worse than Iblis. Lucifer, as the Christian devil is sometimes called, came to the belief that he was stronger than God. This idea of the devil became so strong that he rebelled and attempted to attack God and become the ruling power of the heavens. The story of the first battle between the devil and God is not found in the Christian Bible. His appearance, however, is fully a part of the Bible and we see him as constantly testing and tempting the loyalty of man to the Lord. In our study of the theological views of the devil, we looked at his involvement in man's original sin, and his attempts to tempt both Job and Jesus away from the Lord. As we pointed out, the devil was able to tempt and conquer the mind of man but was unable to conquer the Son of Man. Later, in the Revelation of St. John the Divine, the demise of the devil is also spelled out and his reign of evil is crushed. As Christianity has grown to the level of popularity it is at today, it should come as no surprise that the writings that the religion has produced are monumental. Indeed, the devil has been the subject of some of the writings. As we continue our look at the Bible's view of the devil and its answer to our question, let us explore some Christian writings on the devil and see if they can give us some insight as we attempt to make our own answer.

In our second section, we gave the nuts and bolts of the devil as he appears in the Christian Bible. It gave us a good look at how the devil has throughout the time of man tried to tempt and lure man away from God's graces. It also gave us the

End of Days story with the archangel Michael ending the devil's evil reign upon man. In the Christian Bible, however, it could honestly be said that the devil is the Lord's nemesis. He alone goes against the will of God and his only punishment seems to be his exile from Heaven. In the end he is imprisoned for his evil deeds, but in the meanwhile he is able to run free performing all the evil deeds he wants. The question of why God would allow the devil the freedom to perform such evil deeds is a deep theological question that warrants its own book. Don't worry though, we are not going to go there. As much as the devil would like me to drift off topic and make this work unreadable, I will not fall for his tricks. We will now look at some of the additional Bible passages that mention the devil as well as some of the early Christian writings about the devil that came after the writing of the holy text. As the Christian Bible provides us with a clear struggle between the forces of good and the forces of evil, I believe that not taking a deeper look into the writings of early Christian writers would make our study, and therefore our own answer to the question, woefully uneducated. One might say that I am beginning to tread on some very dangerous paths. It might also seem like I am reaching up to get the fruit from the Forbidden Tree. Not to worry, I have no thoughts of being able to know the plan of God or leading you to believe we are able to do so. As I have said, my quest is simply to provide all the information possible to give us the best possible answer that humans can give to the question. Nothing more. Nothing less. He has tried to drive me away from that ultimate goal, but once again the devil has failed. Let us now pick up the pace and finish our look at the Christian writings about the devil.

While rather blasphemous and perhaps a reason for a fatwa to be declared against me or my excommunication from the church, I will once again try to compare the Qur'an and the Bible to a major Hollywood picture. Before I start to anger anyone, there can truly be no comparison and I will attempt to explain why. The usual Hollywood screenplay follows a three-act structure with plot points, conflicts, and ultimately a resolution. If one were to look at the Qur'an or Bible as strictly works of literature we might say they are both beautifully written but the story is a bit lacking. Although there is conflict between the followers of "good" against the forces of "evil", neither book gives the reader any question as to the ultimate resolution. God wins and the Devil loses. It is all spelled out for the followers of the world's two largest religions, and yet we still find it necessary to go against the words of these spiritual books and ask ourselves whether the devil is winning. Do we commit a sin every time we ask the question? Is the devil actually tempting our souls to the point where we are moving away from the grace of God every time we ask the question? Although I will be in no way able to cause people to stop asking the question, I will give my response to the question in the next section. Perhaps the view of another mortal and failed man may steer people away from questioning God's plan for us and their views of the chances that the devil may be winning. I know this will not be the case, but if my words sway the thoughts of just one person I will have accomplished my goal.

As the term antichrist only appears in the Christian Bible, we will focus our theological look there. As important as we would believe the antichrist to be, the term is only mentioned five times in the Gospel of John. The antichrist is not even mentioned in the Qur'an, although there are sections where something that could be deemed an antichrist emerges from the Earth. As John warns, there are many that will enter the world with the sole purpose of deceiving man and leading him away from God. For John and the Christian Bible, this includes tempting man to deny that Jesus is in fact the Messiah and the Son of God. This passage does make it clear that deceivers do walk amongst us, but those who follow the Muslim faith may view it as an attack on them. While the passage does claim that those who deny that Jesus is the Savior and Son of God are antichrists, a deeper look at the second epistle of John does provide all of man with important guidance. "Little children, it is the last time: and as ye have heard that antichrist shall come, even now are there many antichrists; whereby we know that it is the last time." It is from this passage that all of man is warned that antichrists do walk the Earth spreading confusion and evil in their wake. Although this passage is from the Christian Bible, it makes no distinctions on man. We are all called to keep an eye out for false deceivers and antichrists and prepare for the end of days. The passage makes no distinctions, although coming from the Christian Bible, the natural assumption is that it is for followers of God the Father and Jesus His Son. If we look at the passage with a blind eye to its religious origin we can see that it is good for all man. We can have no doubt that evil walks amongst us and every man has a responsibility to reject such forces. As we finish our look at theological sources, let us now travel to medieval Europe.

St. Thomas Aquinas was a thirteenth century priest whose teachings shaped modern theology and stay with us today. His teachings are actually still used by those studying for the priesthood. Known as a teacher of the faith, it should come as no surprise that he also dealt with the devil and his influence on the world and man. St. Thomas Aquinas argues that there are two spiritual bodies working on Earth- the body of Jesus Christ and the body of the devil. He also states that the body of Jesus is the Church. His studies on the body of the devil resemble the theme of this book. He makes the argument that just as the apostles and the modern church are always looking to introduce new souls to the goodness and glory of Jesus Christ, the devil is also looking to lure man away from Jesus to build the strength of his body on earth. Each soul that is lured away by the devil makes his body on earth stronger while the earthly form of Jesus's body- the church- weakens.

In the time of St. Thomas Aquinas the church was still trying to spread the message of Jesus to the people of the world. Although the new world had yet to be discovered, there were still a multitude of people who had not been introduced to the ministry of Jesus Christ. If we were to look at his teachings strictly from the narrow view of the historical context, we would say that St. Thomas Aquinas was pushing the missionaries of the time to increase the scope of Jesus' ministry, strengthen his body on Earth, and weaken the devil's influence on man. As we have said, however, the teachings of St. Thomas Aquinas are still used today. Far from a theological debate, the reason is that his teachings are equally as important eight hundred years after his death. In his time, the ministry of Jesus and the promise of salvation were not as well-known as they are today. While the ministry of Jesus is now known throughout the world, the mission of the devil to strengthen his Earthly power is ignored by many. Reading his works nine centuries later, we can understand why St. Thomas Aquinas reached sainthood and is considered one of the great teachers of the Church. Just as relevant today, the writings of St. Thomas Aquinas can be used by everyday people as they strive to fight the devil and receive the ultimate salvation that Jesus has provided us. Once again, it asks us to use our free will to determine whether we are strengthening the body of Christ on Earth or giving the devil extra strength. Although the above passages do not mention the end of days, they do tell us not to fall away from the grace of God and to move towards the devil.

The nature of the devil and the angels that reside in heaven have long intrigued us. Before St. Thomas Aquinas, there were the writings of Augustine, Dionysius, and John of Damascus which all took a look at the structure of the angelic order as well as the fallen angel Satan. While man has struggled to determine the nature of the devil and how to identify his evils, not even St. Thomas attempts to tell us who the antichrist is and his answer to the question of this book would of course follow the Biblical answer. As we look at the men of theology who have studied the nature of evil and its effects on man we once again do not receive the answer we so crave. The very difficult thing with religion is that most of the time we need to rely on our faith. It is in difficult times like the ones we currently find ourselves in when our faith may be shaken. It is times like this when we start to seriously consider the unimaginable- Is the devil winning?

One would think that the spiritual guides that will lead us to eternal salvation would also provide us with some sort of instruction on who the antichrist is, how to identify him, and how to reject the evil that the antichrist promotes. This is, once again, a misuse of the free will that God has given man. The Bible makes references to the antichrist so that man knows and understands that there will be those who will try to lure him away from God. The theological sources are indeed books filled with laws to assist man to reach salvation, but it is an error to think that God did not know that some men would fall from the way. Did God know that the first man would fall from grace and eat of the forbidden fruit? Of course He did. It is just another sign of the love that God has for us that He allows man to make the occasional stumble and yet still have the opportunity to join Him in Heaven. It is the love that God has for us that

He has the trust in man to be able to identify the "antichrist" and reject his evil ways. Man might even be tricked into saying that God has put His trust in man in error. God, however, does not have the failings of mortal man. The infallible nature of God should never be questioned, nor should His ultimate plan. Yet it cannot be denied that man steadily falls for the evils of men that history has called the "antichrist". As we conclude the book, we will look to these men who showed all the qualities of an antichrist and attempt to answer the question this book asks.

VI

We find ourselves coming to the end, and still no closer to answering the question. Yes, we are now much more informed to the devil's tricks, but we are not now, nor ever will be, in a position to truly answer the question. The divine ways are not the ways of mortal man and we should not fool ourselves into thinking otherwise. The stain of original sin that was caused when Adam and Eve disobeyed in order to gain the knowledge of God still dirties us. Still, the question is out there begging for an answer. I promised that I would give as good of an answer as a mortal could give. If this were a TV show instead of a book, this would be an excellent time to cut to a commercial. Fortunately for my readers there are no commercial breaks in books, so here is my answer. Is the devil winning? My answer is an emphatic no. I know that may seem like the cop out answer of a God fearing mortal. I do not deny that I live my life trying not to disappoint God and trying to stay in his grace. What I will say is that my answer to the question is a direct result of my free will, my research on the matter, and my own personal opinion. I hope that by reading this far you know me enough to realize that the emphatic "no" will not be the end of my answer. As we finish, I will try to explain why this is my answer as well. I also hope it will be yours as well. In the books beginning, I showed how the devil has transformed in an almost cartoonish figure. I believe that there is still that fear of the devil in our hearts and that people increasingly asking if he is winning is just proof of our fear. We have now, however, also started to look for the man who is the harbinger of the end of days.

The antichrist. As previously mentioned, only the Christian Bible names this antagonist for Jesus our Savior, and the idea of an "antichrist" only appears five times in the Gospel of John. Man has become, however, intrigued by the thought that there may be one amongst us who will usher in the End of Days. Much like how we have described the change in man's view of the devil, so we have also seen a change in the views of the antichrist. Although the antichrist has not taken on the "cute" images that the devil has in popular culture, it cannot be denied that the antichrist has become a somewhat popular term for describing someone who is deemed "evil". From books to movies to cable television specials, it seems that we as man have an almost sinful obsession with finding out who the antichrist is. We call politicians we do not like the antichrist. Serial killers are often called the antichrist. In our own lives, we read the texts of a 16th century man who purported to tell the future. We look for the three "antichrists" he says will appear and wonder if some have already spread their evil upon the earth and man. This is actually a quite important thing I need to look at to verify my answer to the question. If "antichrists" have walked amongst us, can there be any question as to whether the devil is indeed taking the upper hand? In the next few parts we will explore the truly evil people in recent history who have been called the antichrist. By exploring their evil ways and their demises, I hope to not only refute the antichrist claims but strengthen my answer to the question.

There can be no question that men of an almost incarnate evil have walked the earth. The question then becomes "Are any of these men the antichrist who will bring us to the End of Days?" We will look at three men who all have been called the antichrist (with good reason). It is by looking at these men who were considered the ultimate evil that we can explore whether they were simply pawns in the devil's quest to bring his evil upon the earth or a greater part of the devil's twisted scheme. The first man we will look at is Joseph Stalin, whose run as the General Secretary of the Soviet Union not only led to the strengthening of the communist state but also caused the deaths of millions of his own people. Stalin is an interesting subject for this book because the evil he propagated was upon his own people. Although the age of nuclear weapons meant that the Soviet Union had a forty year reign of striking terror and fear into the hearts of man, the true terror of Stalin was felt in "Mother Russia". Although the secretive Soviet society did not keep such records- nor would they be deemed as reliable if they did- it is estimated that the lives that were lost because of Stalin's rule dwarf that of the Nazi holocaust. Let us now take a close look at the evil that was Joseph Stalin. The General Secretary and Premier of the Soviet Union. The purported cause of tens of millions of deaths. The antichrist?

Perhaps the greatest evil perpetrated by Stalin is the use of the government agency that became known as the Gulag. This government agency ran forced labor camps. Although it publically stated that those who were sent to the labor camps were prisoners, they were also filled with men who the government considered to be politically opposed to the Soviet regime. In the secret circles that was the Soviet Union, it is difficult to even attempt to get an accurate number of how many people were sent to these labor camps. The accounts from those lucky enough to survive the labor camps have told us about the terrible conditions that led to a multitude of deaths. Prisoners had to endure twenty hour work days with limited food rations. Although the work accomplished under these conditions was not the quality or quantity as that performed by "free" laborers, the Gulag maintained these camps for forty years. We will never know the number of deaths caused by these forced labor camps, but it is safe to say that the number is monumental. As the scope of the Soviet Union increased, so did the evilness of Stalin's rule. The Soviet Union controlled what was known as the "eastern bloc" and as it expanded Communist control over other countries it demanded allegiance by using any means possible. The Ukraine was a prime example of the evil that Stalin promoted. The country was rich with farmland, but in order to fund the Soviet Union the grain was sold off while the Ukrainian people starved. The number of deaths caused by Stalin's forced famine exceeds that of the Jewish holocaust.

It is hard to argue that the actions of Stalin led directly to the deaths of millions and indirectly to the deaths of many more after his own death. But is he the antichrist? Stalin died in 1952 as a result of his heavy smoking. The question then becomes- If Stalin was indeed the antichrist why did the Soviet Union continue without him after his death and why did it eventually crumble? It cannot be denied that Stalin was the personification of evil in his lifetime and that there are still people today who revere the fallen leader. We are, however, looking at Stalin in a much deeper tone than just the admiration of man. If one studies the Bible, it can be said that Stalin did in fact have some qualities of an antichrist. In fact, it would not be wrong to call Stalin an antichrist. But "the" antichrist? Stalin has been dead for sixty years, and although we consider the present to be wrought with evil, it would be a stab in the dark to place the blame on Stalin. He was without a doubt evil and the cause of the deaths of millions- but does that make Stalin the antichrist?

Before we answer that question let us move to another figure in recent history who many believe might have been "the" antichrist. Adolph Hitler. The leader of the Nazi party which caused the Second World War, the defining force that led to the genocide of six million Jews, and a man who struck fear in the world for almost a decade- Hitler was considered the ultimate in evil. The entire European Continent was in fear of Hitler and his Nazi army as it pursued its blitzkrieg attempt to control every inch of Europe. These invasions served a number of purposes for Hitler. First, it expanded the reach of his desired "perfect race". Secondly, it kept the world's attention away from the evils that were being done in Nazi Germany. Finally, it took all the attention off of the Nazi death camps. With the evil that evolved under Hitler's direction, it would not be an unrealistic claim to say that Hitler was the antichrist. He certainly used all the devil's weapons against his fellow man. Countries that found themselves in his crosshairs were in a constant fear of the Nazi army. People in the counties occupied by the Nazis and those in the death camps were in a daily fear for their lives. The greed for power was seen within the people of the Nazi Party. Following Hitler's orders, there was no evil they would not commit to cement their power. Once again, the forces of "evil" seemed poised to conquer the forces of "good". Of course, the War was first waged due to Hitler's lightning expansion across the European Continent. The call, used too much these days, was that democracy needed to be protected. As Japan had attacked Pearl Harbor and Hitler was steamrolling his way through Europe, the argument for defending democracy was a valid one. It perhaps led the way for preserving democracy being a reason for future wars, but few can question whether World War 2 was fought for a good cause. As the Allies pushed into Europe and made their way to Germany it became quite clear this war was being fought for more than the preservation of democracy. It was a war to destroy evil.

Most of the evils that were performed under Stalin were hidden under the strict privacy of the Soviet Union. Even as the Soviet Union crumbled, the secrets it held may have slowly leaked out but have never been completely disclosed. As

Communism fell, however, Russia remained a strong nation and the Communists who ran the U.S.S.R. still closely guard the secrets of the communist reign of the country. Hitler, however, was never looking for a peaceful resolution. His quest- perhaps fueled by insanity, perhaps fueled by the devil- was always to take over the world with his "perfect" German race. As the Allied forces found as they began their march towards Berlin, there was little evil that the Nazis would not do to accomplish their goal. Soviet forces were the first to come across an abandoned death camp. As they reached the abandoned and burned camp, the gas chamber still remained and was the first proof that the rumors of the atrocities of the Nazis was indeed a reality. As the Allies pushed in from the west, the enormity of the evil became a frightening reminder of why the world needed to stop Adolph Hitler and Nazi Germany. We would later learn that the Nazi Party was responsible for the deaths of millions of people whose only crime was the fact that they were Jewish. Add to that the number of people killed because they did not meet the standard for Hitler's "perfect race" and the number of people killed jumps. The commonly stated number for Jews killed in the holocaust is six million, although with all the other groups that were affected there have been estimates that put the number as high as twenty million people that might have lost their lives due to the evils of Nazi Germany.

My paternal grandfather was a 37 year old private in the army during WW2 when he got the call that his unit was going to join the fight in Europe. It was 1944, and the tide of the war was turning to the side of the Allies, but Hitler was going to put up one last stand. The Battle of the Bulge was a fierce battle that Hitler expected to win. The Soviets were quickly advancing toward Germany and as he considered the Western Allied powers to be weaker than their Soviet counterparts, he focused his attention to the Ardennes as opposed to the charging Soviet forces. My grandfather, Andrew Leonard, was killed as a member of the Allied forces of the west. These forces not only repelled the Nazi offensive, but began to storm into Germany. Hitler was in everyone's crosshairs as the Soviets came from the east and the Americans came from the west. The amount of deaths in the Battle of the Bulge was the highest in any battle fought in WW2, but it opened the door to Berlin and cemented the end of Hitler's reign of terror. With the Soviet forces steadily approaching his position, and the American forces blocking any escape route, this man of pure evil took the easy way out. On April 30th, 1945, Adolph Hitler committed suicide and in effect the "Third Reich" ceased to exist. As a man who had been the leader of Germany for over ten years, the news of his death did not cause a great outpouring of emotion from the German people. There was little, if any, remorse. The end was finally here.

The question, then, is whether Adolph Hitler was in fact the antichrist. As we know, the terror and evil that he caused was so extreme that it is no wonder why people may consider him to be the antichrist. Skinheads and Neo-Nazis tell us that the evil effects of Hitler remain with us to this day. The evil he left upon the Earth would no doubt cause him to be compared to the devil and the fact that he was eventually linked to the antichrist was just a natural aftereffect as we saw the images of the survivors liberated from the death camps and learned of the amount of people he killed. But was Hitler the antichrist? Like Stalin, Hitler's deeds without a doubt make him one of the most evil men in history. This leads us to question just how evil he actually was. We can look at how the Nazi way was crushed with his death, whereas Stalin's Communism continued to rule Russia for decades after his passing. I believe it is also important to look at the nature of Hitler's death before we anoint him as the antichrist. Soviet forces had entered Berlin and were but a few blocks away when Hitler put his pistol to his head and pulled the trigger. Would Hitler be the antichrist if he worried that his power was soon to be finished? Would the fear of the devil terrorize him as Soviet forces were about to take him if he were the antichrist? If Adolph Hitler was "the" antichrist he did a terrible job. At the time of his death, he was hated- even by those in his own country. I thought the antichrist would help the devil by turning man away from God. I guess Hitler didn't get the memo, or more likely he was not the antichrist.

Our question asks if the devil is now winning, and there is no doubt that we now find ourselves in the midst of a man that even after his death is called the harbinger of the end of times. Usama bin Laden. The antichrist? The founder of the terrorist group Al Qaeda and architect of the 9/11 attacks on America, bin Laden met all the criteria for the antichrist. He spread the devil's weapon of fear to every inch of the world. His lies and deceptions have led countless people away from the grace of God. Thousands of innocent lives were lost as a direct result of the terror that bin Laden and Al Qaeda performed throughout the world. Unlike the first two, bin Laden added a new element to his evil. He claimed to be doing the work of Allah and that he was defending all Muslims from infidels of the faith. In recruiting for Al Qaeda, he also went after the weak in society and recruited them into his terror organization by giving them the false promise of Allah's happiness with their actions. It also played on the weakness of man by giving them a sense of power they never had. By combining the terror he was spreading with man's desire to please Allah, bin Laden was able to build a fearsome and well spread terror group. A group that would change the entire world- and not for the better.

Usama bin Laden and Al Qaeda were long a thorn in the side of the western world. Annoying and sometimes painful and deadly, the forces of Al Qaeda began its quest to attack those deemed "evil" by bin Laden by carrying out attacks on overseas American targets. Although we did not consider them small scale attacks at the time, the destruction and loss of life that these attacks produced were small in comparison to the future Al Qaeda attacks. The attacks on the USS Cole and various U.S. embassies in Africa brought anger to the American public, but being half a world away brought little fear. Even the first attack carried out with the assistance of Al Qaeda on the World Trade Center in 1993 brought more anger than fear upon the American people. If I remember correctly, there was no mention of Al Qaeda after the first WTC attacks. We were shown a blind sheikh who was the mastermind of the attack. While he was the leader of a separate group of Egyptian Muslim militants, Al Qaeda did have a hand in the attacks. A full eight years before the 9/11 attacks, Al Qaeda already had a network of militant training camps. The man who carried out the bombing on the WTC had attended one of Al Qaeda's training camps in Afghanistan. As would be seen with many terrorist attacks that followed, bin Laden and Al Qaeda seemed to always have a hand in any terrorist attacks. Two things we do know for sure is that bin Laden and Al Qaeda were increasing their strength every day and that bin Laden's plans were growing in the scale of their evilness. The evils of the man and the reasons why people call him the antichrist would explode upon the world in September, 2001.

We began the book by detailing the horror of the events of September 11th, and I do not think it serves us any purpose to rehash those horrible events. It is important, though, to look at the attacks as the horrible way bin Laden was able to cement his role as the leader of Al Qaeda and as a man who would strike fear into the world. Since bin Laden and his terror group were able to successfully attack the mainland of the United States by destroying two landmarks that defined the skyline of New York City, there seemed to be no limit to the evil that bin Laden possessed. In our new media managed society and the explosion of the Internet, he was able to continually strike fear into man with his short videos promoting the Al Qaeda cause and pushing for more attacks. The free world made every attempt to crush Al Qaeda, but the group grew and now had bases in many smaller and impoverished Muslim countries. Al Qaeda cells were discovered and destroyed on American soil. No matter how hard countries seemed to fight back, the nature of Al Qaeda kept its terror alive. The attention that it now garnered was a double-edged sword. Yes, the ability of the group to pull off terror events the scope of the 9/11 attacks was severely hampered, but the attacks gave the group leverage to increase it ranks upon the disenfranchised members of third world countries. Although here in America we believed the country was now guarding itself against any further attacks, we knew that Al Qaeda was as strong as ever. Since then a shoe bomber was captured before he could ignite the explosive and take down another plane and we knew that more attempts would be made. Then there was the ever-present elephant in the room. Usama bin Laden, founder of Al Qaeda and architect of the 9/11 attacks, was still free to work his evil.

As the years passed after 9/11, capturing or killing bin Laden seemed to take a backseat to destroying Al Qaeda. We were told that bin Laden was no longer in control of Al Qaeda and was now just a symbolic leader in hiding. It was also leaked that U.S. forces had come within minutes of his location before he got away. It seemed like bin Laden had become the terrorist version of Tom Joad. If there was an embassy bombing- he was there. A terrorist with a suicide vest kills dozens- he was there.

Of course, bin Laden was never in any of those places or a part of any of those events, but like Tom Joad and the persecuted, the spirit of bin Laden was present in all those events. The prevailing thought became that bin Laden would never be found. The media, and therefore the mindless sheep that follow their word as law, resigned itself to the "fact" that the man responsible for the worst terrorist attack on American soil would live to old age as a free man. I woke up on May 3rd, 2011, and got ready for work with no idea of what had happened the night before. As I was walking to my car I saw a newspaper that had been delivered. I had to give it a second look as I could not believe my eyes. BIN LADEN DEAD. I rushed to my car and turned on the news radio station. It was true. The Navy Seals had performed a raid in Pakistan that resulted in the death of Usama bin Laden. Al Qaeda and its terror still stood, but the face of evil had been destroyed.

Bin Laden resembled Biblical and theological views of the antichrist much more than the previous two men we mentioned. Whereas Stalin and Hitler took their nations away from religious belief, bin Laden used the Islamic religion and turned it around to use as a pawn to promote his evil ways. It would be hard to say that bin Laden stayed on Allah's straight path to salvation but rather veered off course to the path where the devil resides. In the end, however, bin Laden was dealt the same fate as Stalin and Hitler. He was killed and life continued. Yes, Al Qaeda and the fear of terrorism still remains, but the terror that the face of bin Laden gave the world is now sitting in the bottom of some sea. The horror of bin Laden stays with us to this very day, but so do the horrors caused by Stalin and Hitler. They stay with us, but do they conquer us? The Communist reign of Russia collapsed. The genocide of the Jews was a failure. The deaths of Bin Laden and other leaders has left Al Qaeda weakened and in a general state of disarray. Were any of those men more than simple pawns in the devil's high stakes chess game against God? I know that many will still claim that these men were "the" antichrist, but I must disagree. While these men were the definition of evil, it is hard to say that these mortal lives affected the spiritual battle of good versus evil. All three men find themselves subject to hatred after their deaths. Their way of living is now despised as pure evil. Seeing how the evil of these men is reviled, how is the question becoming such an increasing question asked by everyday people?

Eternal salvation and joining God in paradise should be everyone's goal, but as we have seen man is easily turned away from following the path necessary to achieve everlasting life with God. From Adam and Eve in Eden to the greed of major corporations and the people that run them today, it is obvious that man has not learned his lesson. My personal opinion is that perhaps asking the question is simply another failing of man. We now live in a world where "It wasn't me" and "It was like that when I got here" prevails over taking responsibility for one's actions. Politicians deny any improprieties until the evidence against them becomes too tremendous for their denials to hold water. Athletes deny that they are taking steroids or PEDS until a positive test proves their guilt. This is, unfortunately, the world we live in. It may be easy to point the finger at the rich and powerful, but it is never easy to point the finger at ourselves. I have looked at my own life and failings before looking at those of my fellow man as I attempt to show that the answer to the question of this book is and always was

"No" and that it may just be our excuse for not asking the real question- "Are we losing?"   As difficult as it is to look in the mirror and question ourselves, it is the only way we can truly answer whether it is man failing God or the devil winning.

A mirror.   A common object found in almost every American house that provides a reflective image of whatever is in front of it. As mankind has advanced it has become quite a useful tool in society. How else could we know we have a snot hanging out our nose or if our hair is sticking up? Writing that was just another example for me of where mankind has fallen to. Saving ourselves from embarrassment and styling ourselves to meet the expectations of society have become the keys to many people's lives. As this simple piece of glass is used to increase the vanity of man, it is also used as a device that brings about depression and self-hating. I know that many readers will think that I am talking about women here. Yes, women are prone to self-deprecation in the mirror image of themselves, but men cannot fool themselves into thinking that this is just "a woman's problem".   When I look in the mirror do I see myself as other people do? I see an unattractive, underweight, mess. Now, I understand that I am underweight and do not feel that is a negative factor. The other things I see, though, are nothing but negatives. I am not good looking. It is the face of failure. I see a look of depression and I understand why. I see a face devoid of hope and I feel forced to agree with it. Not a great way to start the day, but I am sure that multitudes start their days the very same way. It is funny how a piece of glass can lead us away from the fact that we are God's children who were made in His image. Well, it is not funny at all but rather an unfortunate truth. Although this is not exactly what I mean when I say perhaps we need to look in the mirror to find the answer to our question, it is without a doubt a good start. If a simple mirror can lead us away from thinking we were made in God's image, what else could we learn from this simple item we now take for granted?

We have explored the weapons that the devil uses in his quest to lead man against God and strengthen his chances in his ultimate end of days battle against the Lord. Money (the green tea) and oil (the black tea) have indeed led man away from the grace of God. As we were trying to answer the question "Is the devil winning?" it should come as no surprise that our study has come with blinders on. Perhaps my own fault- but perhaps what needed to be written- we have focused on how the devil uses these weapons to deceive man. I mentioned that the world we now live in has become a world where man has an increasing tendency to shirk responsibility and pretend that the evils they act upon are not real. This may upset some readers, but that hole in the ozone and the denials of its causes are a prime example of this. No matter how many scientists say that the hole is caused by man spreading ozone destroying pollution across the Earth, there are still people who deny that an increasing use of CFCs has aided our ozone's depletion. I guess the profits caused by refrigerants and other CFCs are large enough for them to conveniently ignore and deny the effects on our planet. There are many other subjects where the "it wasn't me" nature of man has damaged both mankind and their relationship with God, but I think this is a good point to get back to our mirror. The piece of glass that leads many to depression because their vision is so clouded by societal norms that they do not see that they are in fact beautiful. The piece of glass that becomes so cloudy that man thinks that his monetary success makes him a good person.

With our study of the green tea and the black tea, we placed our focus on how the devil used the items of money and oil to coerce men to perform evil and go against the will of God. We showed how the devil was able to change with the times and use the growth of both imperialism and capitalism as well as the growing need for crude oil to his advantage. In each section, I talked about how the devil unleashed his weapons upon man. Please notice that there is always one constant in both of the "teas". MAN. Man was all too willing to send armies to their death in order to gain more wealth and power. Man was willing to put his fellow man in an impossible position to profit from predatory loans. Man was willing to do whatever it took for him to fulfill his selfish needs. The story of Adam and Eve shows us the origin of original sin and man's fall from God. Have we once again fallen like the first man for the devil's tricks? In the story of the Garden of Eden, the devil presents himself to Eve and in that way is able to tempt man away from God and into sin. Once they are thrown out of the Garden, man knows good and evil. Man should know the ways the devil tries to trick him. Yet, all it takes is a simple nudge and we fall right back off the wagon. But we still question whether the devil is winning. I think I need to start handing out mirrors.

The two texts of the world's major religions have different end of day stories, but both end with the failure and destruction of the evil force known as the devil. In the Qur'an, Iblis keeps his end of the deal with Allah and voluntarily goes into the abyss that is hell. In the Bible, Satan wages a war against God and is defeated by the archangel Michael and imprisoned in the abyss. As we have said, more than half of the world's population are followers of these two religions. Religions that quite clearly answer the question this book asks in their sacred texts. Being a Christian, I know how the Bible is dissected and analyzed by multitudes of sources. I personally take the Old Testament as mostly parables meant to show us the way to follow the will of God and a guide to joining Him in Paradise. My view of the New Testament and the gospels is that the ministry of Jesus and his mission to save man are absolute fact. I take the New Testament as every word being true. I believe that Jesus came here to save the souls of man and defeat the evils of the devil. More importantly, I know that Jesus could never be defeated in this mission. With that being said, I think my answer to the question is quite clear. The devil is not winning, nor was that ever a possibility. With all of the research I have done, to me it has become very clear that we are asking the wrong question. The devil is not winning, but are we losing?

I know it is difficult, but I also know how important it is to now turn the mirror around and stop looking for the devil's evil ways and to start looking at our own. The devil has no power except that which is given to him by man. If we were able to harness the good of our free will, what power would the devil have over us? What power would the devil have at all? The devil, while still one of God's angels (albeit a fallen angel), has already shown us that he has no power over God. From his initial defeat and expulsion from Heaven to his failure in his attempts to tempt Jesus away in the desert, it has always been clear that the devil and his "power" are nothing compared to the power of the Lord. Tempting humans to join him in the ultimate battle is the only way the devil could believe that he even has a chance. As the failure of man has grown to unseen proportions, the devil has seen his army against the forces of

God become immense. With the pride of the devil, he may actually think that this time his battle against God will have a different outcome. He may think that he will be on a throne as master of the heavens. Unfortunately for the devil, he will never have the power to conquer God. He will never see the glory of Heaven again. Perhaps, however, the most unfortunate thing is what will happen to those who have been fooled by the devil's tricks. Those who have fallen from the way of God will take up arms with the devil in an unwinnable attempt to hold their Earthly power, their BMWs, and their hefty bank accounts. In the end they will not have any of these earthly pleasures and they will watch paradise pass them by as they take residence in the abyss of Hell.

Is the devil winning? No. Is mankind losing? Maybe. We have spent the entire book looking at the tricks and deceptions that the devil uses against man. We have looked at how money and oil have brought out the worst in man and placed the blame solidly on the devil. While we cannot deny that the devil has had a hand in this with his deceptions, I think that it is an error to place the blame totally on the devil. It makes no difference to the devil if we blame him. He has already been thrown out of paradise and his only chance to regain entrance is to build his army of mortal souls for his ultimate attack on God. Our study of the Bible tells us that this attack is doomed to fail, but much like the mortals the devil loves to deceive his pride is too great to accept this fact. Our study on the events that have occurred in both the history of mankind and the present has shown us that man's pride and greed can often be so great that it leads us away from paradise.

The devil had everything. He was one of God's angels and resided in Heaven. He was able to enjoy the fruits of Paradise with the Lord and chose not to. Adam and Eve ate from the fruit of the forbidden tree and it can be argued that mankind chose not to be in Paradise with God. The first man regretted his original sin, but the stain of that sin would forever be upon us. As the parable of the prodigal son taught us, however, it is never too late to return to our Father's house. God sent his only Son to Earth to open the gates of Heaven for mankind when the end is here. As we do not know when the End of Days will be upon us, I can only strongly suggest that we all look into that mirror and take an honest look at ourselves and ask the question if we are failing God. God will never fall so the question is really whether we are going to fall alongside the devil.

Oh, and for all those who have been faithfully reading, I was able to sneak a peek over God's shoulder to see the cards he is holding. Four kings. He sits holding his cards, showing no emotion as the devil gloats over his four jacks. Satan is in for a shock when the End of Days come. God will show his hand and give us the definitive answer to our question. Is the devil winning? Not a chance.

References

i-   The 9/11 Commission Report, National Commission on Terrorist Attacks, W. W. Norton & Company; First Edition (July 22, 2004)

ii-   World Mythology, Rosenberg, Donna, McGraw-Hill; 2 edition (January 11, 1994)

The Koran, translated by NJ Dawood, Penguin Books (1990)

The Bible (King James Version)

iii-   Balance- The Economics of Great Powers From Ancient Rome to Modern America, Hubbard, Glenn and Kane, Tim, Simon and Shuster (2013)

Reckless Endangerment, Morgenson, Gretchen & Rosner, Joshua, Times Books, Henry Holt and Company, LLC (2011)

iv-   Oil- Money, Politics, and Power in the 21st Century, Bower, Tom, Grand Central Publishing First Edition (2010)

v-   The Koran, translated by NJ Dawood, Penguin Books
(1990)

The Bible (King James Version)

Aquinas's Shorter Summa: Saint Thomas's Own
Concise Version of His Summa Theologica, St. Thomas
Aquinas, Sophia Inst Pr (2001)

vi-   Hitler and Stalin: Parallel Lives, Bullock, Alan, Vintage
Books (1993)

Ghost Wars: The Secret History of the CIA,
Afghanistan, and Bin Laden, from the Soviet Invasion to
September 10, 2001, Coll, Steve, Penguin Books (2004)